499 FACTS ABOUT HIP-HOP HAMILTON AND THE REST OF AMERICA'S FOUNDING FATHERS

499 FACTS ABOUT HIP-HOP HAMILTON AND THE REST OF AMERICA'S FOUNDING FATHERS

STEPHEN SPIGNESI

Skyhorse Publishing

Skyhorse Publishing books may be purchased in bulk at special discounts for sales promotion, corporate gifts, fundraising, or educational purposes. Special editions can also be created to specifications. For details, contact the Special Sales Department, Skyhorse Publishing, 307 West 36th Street, 11th Floor, New York, NY 10018 or info@skyhorsepublishing.com.

Skyhorse® and Skyhorse Publishing® are registered trademarks of Skyhorse Publishing, Inc.®, a Delaware corporation.

Visit our website at www.skyhorsepublishing.com.

10 9 8 7 6 5 4 3 2 1

Library of Congress Cataloging-in-Publication Data is available on file.

Cover design by Brian Peterson
Cover photo credit: Public domain and iStock

Special Markets Hardcovers ISBN: 978-1-5107-4136-8
Paperback ISBN: 978-1-5107-1212-6
Ebook ISBN: 978-1-5107-1213-3

Printed in the United States of America

This is for Mike, Amy, Samantha, & Sydney Lewis with much love, as well as great admiration for their gumption.

CONTENTS

Part II

AN INVALUABLE 20 FOUNDERS   79

ACKNOWLEDGMENTS

*Special thanks to two people who have
played a role in keeping me writing for quite
some time now:*

Mike Lewis & John White

*Plus, sincere gratitude and abundant love
to the rest of my cherished team—confidantes and boosters all . . .*

My dearest Valerie, my mother Lee, my sister Janet Spignesi Daniw, my beloved Uncle Steve, my cousins Gayze and Judi, my dear friends Dave and LeeAnn Hinchberger, Jim Cole, and George Beahm; plus all of my students, past and present, whose ears I regularly bent with tales of writing and to which they responded politely, and for that, I was always grateful.

*I'd also like to thank my bibliophilic and academic colleagues, along with my
friends at the University of New Haven, especially . . .*

Terry Recchia, Chris Dowd, John Bott, Karen Grava, Hanko Dobi, Lourdes Alvarez, Raeleen Mautner, Mark and Katie McFadden, Kevin Quigley, Sean Patrick Stevens, Don Smith, Rick Farrell, Chuck Timlin, Maura Falise, Diane Spinato, Diane Russo, Randall Horton, Jeff Foster, Wes Davis, Meg Savilonis, Pam Asmus, Andrew Rausch, Anthony Northrup, Lynn Rosano, Molly Seely, Michelle Frankel, John Soltis, Aschlee Riendeau, Nancy McNichol, Cynthia Gwiazda.

Ours is the only country deliberately founded on a good idea.

John Gunther

The American Revolution was a beginning, not a consummation.

Woodrow Wilson

We should keep steadily before our minds the fact that Americanism is a question of principle, of purpose, of idealism, of character; that it is not a matter of birthplace, or creed, or line of descent.

Theodore Roosevelt

The United States has been one of the greatest sources of progress that the world has ever known. We were born out of revolution against an empire. We were founded upon the ideal that all are created equal. And we have shed blood and struggled for centuries to give meaning to those words, within our borders and around the world. We are shaped by every culture. Drawn from every end of the Earth, and dedicated to a simple concept, E pluribus unum: *Out of many, one.*

Barack Obama

INTRODUCTION

Give Props for What They Did!

The Founding Fathers.

Has a nice ring to it, doesn't it? The alliteration, the comforting notion of these iconic men being called "fathers," the conciseness and purity of the message of the phrase.

America's Founding Fathers were, for the most part, visionaries, and men courageous enough to commit treason. (The Founding Mothers—those remarkable women who played a role in the vision quest of establishing America—will be another book at some point.) They rejected the authority of King George and Parliament and set out to conceive a new form of government: the purest, most well-defined republic that ever existed on Earth.

Who were these men? Many consider the term "Founding Fathers" to include well over 100 men. This all-encompassing definition includes those who signed the Declaration of Independence, the Constitution, and the Articles of Confederation.

For purposes of this book, however, we will look mainly at 32 men—the Indispensable 12 and an Invaluable 20—iconic figures who comprised many of the most influential men who participated in the founding of what we today know as the United States of America.

The world may not have seen since a greater assemblage of profound, brilliant, highly educated thinkers committed to a single goal.

What made them Founding Fathers? They were men who decided to invent a new country, a nation that was composed solely of people from other countries, men who decided to write down, for the first time, the idea that everyone is created equal. They also epitomized two noble, enlightened concepts: public service and the greater good.

And if they were around today, I suspect they would probably all be in the Rotary Club, as well as be huge Amazon customers.

But I digress.

There are elements of the story of the Founders and the earliest years of America that have always amazed: what they accomplished under circumstances that today would (generously) be described as primitive. No electricity, writing by hand, no true system of organized medicine, difficult —at best—travel, no real hygiene, and methods of communication that took days, weeks, and sometimes months. (I often ask my students what they think Bach, Mozart, Jefferson, or Franklin would have achieved in a digital world with what's available to us all today. Some perspective always helps, I say.)

Plus, when we consider the fact that everyone back then was almost certainly drunk all the time, as historian Marvin Kittman put it, it was amazing that they could even stand up.

And yet look at what they did!

This book provides a plethora of facts about the Founding Fathers. I hope you find it entertaining, enlightening, educational, and any other positive "e" words you can think of.

Thanks for coming along on this ride into the past.

Stephen Spignesi
New Haven, Connecticut
July 4, 2016

What Are America's Founding Documents?

America's founding documents are the Articles of Confederation, the Declaration of Independence, and the United States Constitution.

Here is a brief look at each of these seminal writings.

The Articles of Confederation

The Articles of Confederation served as the United States' first Constitution. They were adopted by the Continental Congress on November 15, 1777, and were in effect from March 1, 1781, until 1789 when the United States Constitution came into effect.

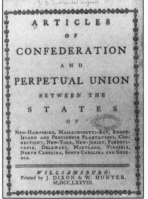

There were only 13 states, but they believed there was a need to codify their existence and validity by writing a set of laws and official policies.

The Articles of Confederation didn't work too well.

What, precisely, was wrong with the Articles of Confederation?

First, they provided no separation of powers. The Articles of Confederation gave each state one vote and a two-thirds majority to pass a law.

They did not give the government the right to collect taxes.

The government couldn't declare or wage war.

The government couldn't even regulate trade.

Essentially, the Articles of Confederation created a weak federal government. Was this intentional? Maybe. A lot of people in the new colonies were still quite skittish about a strong federal government. They'd just left a monarchy, so giving away power to a government was problematic for many.

One of the good things about Articles of Confederation, though, was that they did give us a name: Article I states, "The Stile of this Confederacy shall be 'The United States of America.'" That was the first time we were, so to speak, "official."

And the Articles also served to create a bond among the 13 original states. How is that a bad thing, considering that that initial proclamation of unity resulted in 37 more states over the next century or so?

The Declaration of Independence

It's easy to overlook the importance of the Declaration of Independence. In fact, its name has morphed into a phrase with the words all running together—*declarationofindependence*—and we hardly look at the individual words or consciously suss out their meaning.

Remember that this was a piece of writing to which they had to put a title. They knew their goal: "Hey, Great Britain! We're a sovereign nation, so mess with us at your peril." But what should they call the document that would communicate that message?

Imagine the conversation:

First of all, what is it? It's a statement.
A statement of what?
Individual sovereignty.
So how about The Statement of Individual Sovereignty?
Not very catchy, right?
How about The Statement of Sovereignty?

Kind of boring. And "statement" is kind of weak, isn't it? What's stronger than the word statement? Assertion? Claim? Affirmation? What are we doing with this document?

We're declaring to the world that we are our own country.
Declaring.
So we're making a declaration.
"Declaration" works.
The Declaration of Individual Sovereignty.
Still kind of clunky and wordy. As well as being a mouthful.
So, what actually is individual sovereignty?
Autonomy? The Declaration of Autonomy?
No.
Self-rule?
The Declaration of Self-Rule?
No.
Self-government?
The Declaration of Self-Government?
No. Still too cumbersome.
How about independence? That, after all is what we're declaring, right?
The Declaration of Independence.
Yes! The Declaration of Independence.

That's what we'll call it. And there will be no doubt in King George's chambers as he dons his spectacles and reads the title we have written in a bold hand. It will be clear to see, and it will say what we mean.

Thomas Jefferson wrote the first draft, and notes were provided by John Adams, Benjamin Franklin, and others, and ultimately it evolved into the document known around the world today. Our Declaration of Independence from Great Britain, adopted by Congress in July 1776, has served as an inspiration for other countries and peoples and contains what some have called one of the most well-known sentences in the English language:

> We hold these truths to be self-evident, that all men are created equal, that they are endowed by their Creator with certain unalienable Rights, that among these are Life, Liberty and the pursuit of Happiness.

This sentence begins the second paragraph, though, and in the first paragraph, Jefferson and company rhetorically justify the need for them to make the declaration:

> When in the Course of human events, it becomes necessary for one people to dissolve the political bands which have connected them with another, and to assume among the powers of the earth, the separate and equal station to which the Laws of Nature and of Nature's God entitle them, a decent respect to the opinions of mankind requires that they should declare the causes which impel them to the separation.

King George must have read that and immediately knew what would soon be on his agenda, so to speak. Note Jefferson's word choice: necessary, dissolve, assume, separate, equal . . . these are strong words that contextually set the stage for what's to come.

The United States Constitution

Nascent countries model their constitutions on the United States Constitution, the document that is the supreme law of the United States.

The Constitution defines our federal government as having 3 parts: the executive, the legislative, and the judicial branches.

The legislative is the Congress, consisting of the House of Representatives and the Senate; the executive is the president (yes, the entire executive branch consists of one elected man); the judicial is the federal courts system, culminating with the United States Supreme Court.

The United States Constitution can be amended by the people, but is interpreted by the courts.

The Constitution, as of 2016, is 227 years old, and is still as relevant and important as it was today when it was born in 1789.

The United States Constitution essentially dictates the powers of government. I have a friend, a Constitutional expert, who always says, "The Constitution was not written to protect the government from the people. It was written to protect the people from the government."

The United States Constitution includes the Bill of Rights, one of the most profound documents ever written about freedom, government, and the human condition.

It provides an array of rights that cannot be denied:

- Freedom of speech.
- Freedom of religion.
- Freedom of assembly.
- Freedom of expression.
- The right to bear arms.
- No cruel or unusual punishment.
- The right to a speedy trial.
- No self-incrimination.
- No searches and seizures without a warrant.
- No double jeopardy.
- No trial without an indictment.
- The right to a jury trial.

These are magnificent acknowledgments of our nation's defining principles: all men are created equal, and all men are born free. (See: "What Do the 27 Amendments to the Constitution Do?")

How significant in our history is the United States Constitution?

Significant enough that a TV series, *The West Wing*, devoted an entire storyline to whether or not the original Fifth Amendment has a smudge or a comma in its last line:

Without the comma: "nor shall private property be taken for public use without just compensation."

With the comma: "nor shall private property be taken for public use, without just compensation."

The official government website www.archives.gov presents the text as having the comma.

The United States Constitution is one of the founding documents of the United States, and it might be the single most important document to emerge from the American Revolution.

And not just for Americans.

Docs on the Down Low: Other Important Founding Documents and What They Did

The Articles of Confederation, the Declaration of Independence, and the United States Constitution are the 3 most important founding documents of America. But wait, there's more!

There were other documents that paved the way, set the stage, or reinforced the messages of the Big Three. Here's a look at some of the most important founding documents other than the three we know so well.

The Virginia Statute for Religious Freedom

The first draft of this document was written by Thomas Jefferson in 1777, when he was 34 years old. This document essentially shut down the Church of England's authority over the United States. It became part of Virginia's state law on January 16, 1786.

Catholics, Jews, and miscellaneous Protestants were now all granted the complete freedom to worship as they desired, and they were guaranteed zero intrusion into their belief systems by the government.

Any government.

Obviously, the Virginia Statue for Religious Freedom was the antecedent to the religious freedom rights granted in the First Amendment of the Bill of Rights, except that instead of granting religious freedom to everyone in the country, as the First Amendment did, the Virginia Statute applied only to residents of the state of Virginia.

The Virginia Statute as enacted into law begins:

> Well aware that the opinions and belief of men depend not on their own will, but follow involuntarily the evidence proposed to their minds; that Almighty God hath created the mind free, and manifested his supreme will that free it shall remain by making it altogether insusceptible of restraint . . .

The complete law is 797 words long and the most important section is the second (emphasis added):

> We the General Assembly of Virginia do enact that ***no man shall be compelled to frequent or support any religious worship, place, or ministry whatsoever***, nor shall be enforced, restrained, molested, or burthened in his body or goods, nor shall otherwise suffer, on account of his religious opinions or belief; but that ***all men shall be free to profess, and by argument to maintain, their opinions in matters of religion***, and that the same shall in no wise diminish, enlarge, or affect their civil capacities.

Part I of the law consists of a justification for the law itself. What I have always found fascinating is that Part I of the Virginia Statute might hold the record for the longest run-on sentence in America's historical documents. Part I consists of one *613-word* sentence.

Thomas Jefferson was rarely this long-winded.

The Federalist Papers

The *Federalist Papers* comprised 85 articles and essays written by Alexander Hamilton, James Madison, and John Jay, and they explained and endorsed the ratification of the United States Constitution.

The essays were published in newspapers between October 1787 and August 1788, and they tackled every conceivable issue regarding the establishment of the United States and the need to accept its pending Constitution.

Some of the issues discussed in the *Federalist Papers* included:

- Dangers from foreign countries
- Dangers and consequences from dissension and hostilities between the states
- The importance of preventing insurrection
- The importance of a navy
- Taxes
- The economy
- The problems with the Articles of Confederation
- States' rights
- Checks and balances
- The powers of the Senate
- The Executive department

- How to elect a president
- The powers of the president
- Treaties
- The powers of the judiciary
- Trial by jury

When we consider the differences in how politicians and leaders speak to the masses today and in the period of the *Federalist Papers*, we cannot help but be struck by how effective a seemingly primitive system worked. Thinkers and politicians wrote detailed essays about important issues. The newspapers published them. The citizenry read them.

Today, the Internet provides the identical paradigm, but on an enormously broader scale. And politicians and scholars do use the web to publish important essays and think pieces about our government, socioeconomic climate, our culture, and all manner of topics.

But does anyone read them?

One of the saddest (but most funny) segments comedians and talk show hosts offer is the classic "Man on the Street" interview. They're funny because comedians can make any situation funny. They're very sad because it seems like an awful lot of people today—even with access to the Internet—cannot name the vice president of the United States.

The Northwest Ordinance

The Northwest Ordinance (which was officially known as An Ordinance for the Government of the Territory of the United States, North-West of the River Ohio) basically allowed the new government of the United States to make states. It was ratified on July 13, 1787.

The Northwest Ordinance was the most important act passed under the Articles of Confederation. It established land rights, created the public domain, explained how to add new states to the Union, denoted the rights of citizens of new states *vis à vis* the rights of citizens of existing states, established what essentially became public schools, prohibited slavery in new states, and stated that lands could never be taken away from Indians again.

Part I

The Main Men: 12
Indispensable Founders

George Washington ♦ Thomas Jefferson
♦ John Adams ♦ Benjamin Franklin ♦ James
Madison ♦ Alexander Hamilton ♦ John
Jay ♦ James Monroe ♦ Thomas Paine ♦ Patrick
Henry ♦ Samuel Adams ♦ John Hancock

CHAPTER 1
GEORGE WASHINGTON

The Boss

I have been called upon by the unanimous voice of the Colonies to take command of the Continental Army; an honour I neither sought after, nor desired, as I am thoroughly convinced that it requires greater abilities, and much more experience than I am master of, to conduct a business so extensive in its nature, and arduous in the execution. But the partiality of the Congress, joined to a political motive, left me without a choice; and I am now commissioned a General and Commander-in-Chief of all the forces now raised, or to be raised, for the defence of the United Colonies.[1]

BORN: February 22, 1732 in Westmoreland County, Virginia

DIED: December 14, 1799 in Mount Vernon, Virginia

AGE AT DEATH: 67

CAUSE OF DEATH: Pneumonia. Washington had gone horseback riding in cold, snowy weather, and the following day he complained of a sore throat. This was the beginning of his demise. He was initially diagnosed as suffering from inflammatory quinsy, an inflammation of the tonsils often marked by abscesses. Washington's condition was gravely aggravated by his doctors' "treatments": They bled him with leeches four separate times and raised blisters on his throat and legs as a counterirritant.[2]

POLITICAL PARTY: Federalist Party

FIRST LADY: Martha Dandridge Custis

CAREERS: First president of the United States, 1789-1797, commander-in-chief of the Continental Army, presiding officer of the Constitutional Convention, distiller, planter, real estate investor.

RELIGION: Episcopalian

NICKNAMES: American Fabius, Devourer of Villages (the Iroquois were not fans), the Farmer President, the Father of His Country, the Old Fox, the Potomac Stallion, the Sage of Mount Vernon, the Savior of His Country, the Surveyor President, the Sword of the Revolution, Stepfather of His Country.

MEMORABLE QUOTE ABOUT HIM: "First in war, first in peace, and first in the hearts of his countrymen, he was second to none in the humble and enduring scenes of private life; pious, just, humane, temperate, and sincere; uniform, dignified, and commanding, his example was as edifying to all around him as were the effects of that example lasting." — Congressman Henry Lee

FOUNDING DOCUMENTS SIGNED: The United States Constitution, the New York Ratification of the Bill of Rights

BOOKS TO READ FOR MORE INFORMATION:
- *Washington: A Life* by Ron Chernow
- *His Excellency: George Washington* by Joseph Ellis
- *George Washington: The Indispensable Man* by James T. Flexner
- *The Washingtons: George and Martha, "Join'd by Friendship, Crown'd by Love"* by Flora Fraser
- *George Washington: A Biography* by Washington Irving
- *1776* by David McCullough

We take George Washington for granted in America. We say "He was the father of our country," and everyone nods. He's on the $1 bill. The capital of our country is named after him. The Washington Monument is a globally recognized iconic symbol of America. Yet if there is a single figure who can be called "indispensable" in the epic tale of the birth of the United States of America, it must undoubtedly be George Washington. (Although, ironically, we could also credit another George—King George III—as also being integral to the birth of America. It is, after all, due to him that the colonists fought for their own freedom.)

Washington was indispensable to the formation of the United States of America. He was The Boss. His vision for this new nation was definitive and authoritative. And on top of that, he was a pretty interesting guy as well. He was a planter, a horseman, a brewer . . . and a dancer and gambler, too. (Rumor has it he'd gamble on anything.) Like I said, very cool guy. And his efforts, genius, and commitment resulted in the legacy of the most important, influential, and, yes, indispensable country in the history of the world.

You know that commercial with the guy who's described as "the most interesting man in the world?" Compared to George Washington . . . not even close.

A good illustration of Washington's character and sense of self is the story of his title. After he was inaugurated, it of course came to pass that he needed a title. How should the first president of this new nation be addressed?

One Senate committee came up with the following:

> *"His Highness the President of the United States of America and Protector of the Rights of Same."*

White House history would certainly be different if they had all agreed to that, wouldn't it? But there was one major flaw in this title and that was the fact that we would all be addressing the president as "His Highness." We had just fought a war to rid ourselves of the burden of royal rule, and here we go again: using a term of royalty to describe and address our new president.

Washington himself, it is said, was having none of it. He probably saw that it was quite a malignant contradiction to elevate the leader of the land to a position "higher" than everyone else—in a country founded on the principle that everyone was equal. No one was higher than anyone else. (Bill Maher once had a queen as a guest on his HBO show, *Real Time*. He told the story of how her people gave him strict instructions as to how to address her, how to interact with her, and so forth. They told him he could only address her as "Your Highness." Bill refused and essentially said it was a deal breaker. If she wanted to be on the show, she'd have to allow Bill to address her as he saw fit which, in his case, was by her first name. He made the same point that became an issue with Washington: no one can be defined as a "highness"; i.e., higher than anyone else. The queen was, in the end, on the show.)

Washington wanted to be addressed simply. "Mr. President" would do just fine, he said. And it has for quite some time.

The following section has some interesting facts about G.W., along with some amazing quotes from the American man who was, to all our benefit, utterly indispensable.

16 Things You Never Knew About George Washington

1. George Washington was ambitious, and he wore his military uniform to congressional meetings. This was Washington's silent, and therefore discreet, way of advertising his availability. When John Adams rose to propose Washington be commander-in-chief, Washington left the room so as not to hear what was said about him.

2. When Washington was around 19, he contracted smallpox. He survived the disease, but almost certainly suffered one of the consequences of it later in his life: sterility. He never had biological children with Martha, and historians believe the smallpox, or possibly tuberculosis of the vas deferens, caused his presumed sterility.

24. Do not laugh too loud or too much at any Public Spectacle.

Don't act the fool, part 2.

35. Let your Discourse with Men of Business be Short and Comprehensive.

Don't waste people's time.

38. In visiting the Sick, do not Presently play the Physician if you be not Knowing therein.

Unless you're a doctor, don't act like one.

40. Strive not with your Superiors in argument, but always Submit your Judgment to others with Modesty.

You don't know everything, so don't act like it.

41. Undertake not to Teach your equal in the art himself Professes; it Savours of arrogance.

Don't tell Stephen Hawking about physics, or Stephen King about writing.

3. Washington had several diseases throughout his life, including the aforementioned small pox, plus malaria (at least 5 times), dysentery (at least 3 times), tuberculosis (at least twice), and pneumonia.

4. Historian Peter Henriques in *The Death of George Washington: He Died As He Lived*, said, "Washington died exceedingly hard." He's right.[3]

5. Martha Washington burned her husband's letters after his death. Some survived, however, and later were purchased by the J. P. Morgan Library. J. P. Morgan, taking upon himself the responsibility of destroying writings of the first president of the United States, burned Washington's remaining letters. His reason was that they were "smutty."[4]

6. Slavery did not bring out the best in many people, George Washington included. In 1774, the U.S. capital was moved to Philadelphia and, of course, Washington moved there when he was inaugurated in 1789. At the time, Washington had a slave cook at Mount Vernon named Hercules, who he brought with him to Philadelphia. Washington *really* loved Hercules' cooking, but Pennsylvania law stated that any slave who is brought to the state could only remain enslaved for 6 months. He or she then had to be set free. This did not please George, so he would send Hercules back to Mount Vernon after 5 months or so, let him remain there for a few weeks, and then call him back to Philadelphia where the 6-month clock would start all over again. The resolution of this story is gratifying: Hercules eventually escaped and Washington never saw him again.

7. First President George Washington's salary was $25,000 per year. That was equal to around $615,000 in today's dollars and was, in fact, more than today's U.S. presidents earn. The current presidential salary is $400,000 per year. It's been that amount since 2001, when it was doubled from $200,000. (John Adams, GW's VP, earned $5,000 per year, about $123,000 in today's dollars.)

8. George Washington refused to shake anyone's hand. He felt it was demeaning.

9. George Washington was a prolific writer, but he did not read a lot of books. He did, however, love reading newspapers and subscribed to 10 of them at Mount Vernon.

10. All his life George Washington was afraid of being buried alive. Considering the primitive medical practices of the time, that is actually not an unreasonable fear. On his deathbed, he instructed everyone that he wanted them to wait 2 whole days before burying him, in case they had made a mistake. They waited.

11. George Washington never graduated from college. He was the only Founder who went on to become president who did not have a college degree.

Speaking words of wisdom . . .

12. "I do not conceive we can exist long as a nation, without having lodged somewhere a power which will pervade the whole Union in as energetic a manner, as the authority of the different state governments extend over the several States."[5]

Nobody's perfect? Have you met Donald Trump? Washington disagrees . . .

13. "We must take human nature as we find it, perfection falls not to the share of mortals."[6]

46. Take all Admonitions thankfully in what Time or Place Soever given but afterwards not being culpable take a Time & Place convenient to let him know it that gave them.

Take it with a smile . . . but defend yourself.

47. Mock not nor Jest at any thing of Importance break no Jest that are Sharp Biting and if you Deliver any thing witty and Pleasant abstain from Laughing thereat yourself.

What? You always look perfect? And don't laugh at your own jokes.

48. Wherein you reprove Another be unblameable yourself; for example is more prevalent than Precepts.

When you're ready to blast someone, look in the mirror first.

49. Use no Reproachful Language against any one neither Curse nor Revile.

50. Be not hasty to believe flying Reports to the Disparagement of any.

    Don't believe gossip. You could be the next topic of discussion.

54. Play not the Peacock, looking every where about you, to See if you be well Decked, if your Shoes fit well if your Stockings sit neatly, and Cloths handsomely.

    Don't be vain. Nobody cares.

56. Associate yourself with Men of good Quality if you Esteem your own Reputation; for 'is better to be alone than in bad Company.

    Your friends speak volumes . . . about you!

63. A Man ought not to value himself of his Achievements, or rare Qualities of wit; much less of his riches Virtue or Kindred.

    Don't brag about how incredible you are. Nobody cares.

George liked his alone time . . .

14. "Retired as I am from the world, I frankly acknowledge I cannot feel myself an unconcerned spectator. Yet having happily assisted in bringing the ship into port & having been fairly discharged; it is not my business to embark again on the sea of troubles. Nor could it be expected that my sentiments and opinions would have much weight on the minds of my countrymen—they have been neglected, tho' given as a last legacy in the most solemn manner. I had then perhaps some claims to public attention. I consider myself as having none at present."[7]

GW was really sick of religion . . .

15. "We have abundant reason to rejoice that in this Land the light of truth and reason has triumphed over the power of bigotry and superstition, and that every person may here worship God according to the dictates of his own heart. In this enlightened Age and in this Land of equal liberty it is our boast, that a man's religious tenets will not forfeit the protection of the Laws, nor deprive him of the right of attaining and holding the highest Offices that are known in the United States."[8]

16. "No one would be more zealous than myself to establish effectual barriers against the horrors of spiritual tyranny, and every species of religious persecution."[9]

An Interview with George Washington

What would it be like to sit across from George Washington and interview him in person? What a concept, eh? Perhaps the following "interview" with George Washington (as well as the interviews with the other Founders throughout the book) will be a worthy virtual substitute. These interviews are each a literary patchwork quilt of sorts consisting of questions crafted by myself and my colleagues and answered with the verbatim words of the Founding Father.

We "reverse-engineered" the Founders' words, in a sense, to create what is ultimately a realistic interview with the Founder. The Founders' words were drawn from speeches, writings, and letters and are reproduced precisely as written or uttered. The Founders' words are not edited. We offer this unique perspective as a wish fulfillment exercise: What would it be like to interview George Washington? Hopefully, this will give us a sense of that impossible dream.

Q: Good day, Mr. President. Let's begin with this. What role do you think religion should play in the functioning of our government?

A: As President Madison said, "The civil government functions with complete success by the total separation of the Church from the State."

The foundation of our Empire was not laid in the gloomy age of Ignorance and Superstition, but at an Epocha when the rights of Mankind were better understood and more clearly defined. At this auspicious period, the United States came into existence as a Nation, and if their Citizens should not be completely Free and Happy, the fault will be entirely their own.

Q: Your mother saw you inaugurated as the first president of the United States. She must have been incredibly proud.

A: My mother was the most beautiful woman I ever saw. All I am I owe to my mother. I attribute all my success in life to the moral, intellectual and physical education I received from her.

Q: You've long made it clear, Mr. President, that you oppose cursing, both in public and by the soldiers

64. Break not a Jest where none take pleasure in mirth Laugh not aloud, nor at all without Occasion, deride no mans Misfortune, though there Seem to be Some cause.

Don't make a joke at a funeral.

68. Go not thither, where you know not, whether you Shall be Welcome or not. Give not Advice without being Asked & when desired do it briefly.

Don't crash parties or conversations . . . don't offer advice if not asked for it.

72. Speak not in an unknown Tongue in Company but in your own Language and that as those of Quality do and not as the Vulgar; Sublime matters treat Seriously.

Speak English, or Spanish, or Arabic . . . if that's what everyone is speaking.

73. Think before you Speak pronounce not imperfectly nor bring out your Words too hastily but orderly & distinctly.

Don't come off as ignorant.

79. Be not apt to relate News if you know not the truth thereof. In Discoursing of things you Have heard Name not your Author always A Secret Discover not.

Don't gossip.

80. Be not Tedious in Discourse or in reading unless you find the Company pleased therewith.

Don't be boring.

81. Be not Curious to Know the Affairs of Others neither approach those that Speak in Private.

Don't be nosy.

82. Undertake not what you cannot Perform but be Careful to keep your Promise.

Don't say you can or will do something if you can't or won't.

89. Speak not Evil of the absent for it is unjust.

You wouldn't want to be trashed behind your back, would you?

under your command. Why is this something you feel so strongly about?

A: The foolish and wicked practice of profane cursing and swearing is a vice so mean and low that every person of sense and character detests and despises it.

Q: Even though you feel strongly about profanity, I highly doubt you would want it outlawed. Am I correct?

A: The freedom of speech is taken away, then dumb and silent we may be led away, like sheep to the slaughter.

Q: How would you solve our current problems, specifically foreign entanglement and corrupt politicians?

A: In politics as in philosophy, my tenets are few and simple. The leading one of which, and indeed that which embraces most others, is to be honest and just ourselves and to exact it from others, meddling as little as possible in their affairs where our own are not involved. If this maxim was generally adopted, wars would cease and our swords would soon be converted into reap hooks and our harvests be more peaceful, abundant, and happy.

Q: Do you support borrowing money for capital projects, infrastructure, etc.?

A: As a very important source of strength and security, cherish public credit. One method of preserving it is, to use it as sparingly as possible; avoiding occasions of expense by cultivating peace, but remembering also that timely disbursements to prepare for danger frequently prevent much greater disbursements to repel it; avoiding likewise the accumulation of debt, not only by shunning occasions of expense, but by vigorous exertions in time of peace to discharge the debts, which unavoidable wars may have occasioned, not ungenerously throwing upon posterity the burthen, which we ourselves ought to bear.

Q: How do you think your administration will be judged in the future? And do you believe you made any errors while president?

A: In reviewing the incidents of my administration, I am unconscious of intentional error, I am nevertheless too sensible of my defects not to think it probable that I may have committed many errors. Whatever they may be, I fervently beseech the Almighty to avert or mitigate the evils to which they may tend. I shall also carry with me the hope, that my Country will never cease to view them with indulgence; and that, after 45 years of my life dedicated to its service with an upright zeal, the faults of incompetent abilities will be consigned to oblivion, as myself must soon be to the mansions of rest.

98. Drink not nor talk with your mouth full; neither gaze about you while you are drinking.

Eating or talking with your mouth open is disgusting. Don't do it.

110. Labor to keep alive in your breast that little spark of celestial fire called conscience.

Have a conscience. Karma is real, dudes and dudesses.

The Last Letter George Washington Ever Wrote – and it was to Hamilton

George Washington wrote this letter two days before he died. In it, he discussed with Alexander Hamilton his strong feelings about the creation of a military academy for young boys. He considered the establishment of such an institution to be one of "primary importance."

From George Washington to Alexander Hamilton

December 12, 1799

To Alexander Hamilton

Mount Vernon, December 12th 1799.

Sir,

I have duly received your letter of the 28th ultimo, enclosing a Copy of what you had written to the Secretary of War, on the subject of a Military Academy.

The Establishment of an Institution of this kind, upon a respectable and extensive basis, has ever been considered by me as an Object of primary importance to this Country; and while I was in the Chair of Government, I omitted no proper opportunity of recommending it, in my public Speeches, and otherways, to the attention of the Legislature: But I never undertook to go into a detail of the organization of such an Academy; leaving this task to others, whose pursuits in the paths of Science, and attention to the Arrangements of such Institutions, had better qualified them for the execution of it.

For the same reason I must now decline making any observations on the details of your plan; and as it has already been submitted to the Secretary of War, through whom it would naturally be laid before Congress, it might be too late for alterations, if any should be suggested.

I sincerely hope that the subject will meet with due attention, and that the reasons for its establishment, which you have so clearly pointed out in your letter to the Secretary, will prevail upon the Legislature to place it upon a permanent and respectable footing. With very great esteem & regard I am, Sir, Your most Obedt Servt

Go: Washington

What Washington Ate: Christmas Dinner at Mount Vernon

Check out this bill of fare for a typical Christmas dinner at Mount Vernon when Washington was alive and living there. This is a big meal, no doubt. (All spellings are original. With thanks to Mount Vernon.)

- An Onion Soup Call'd the King's Soup
- Oysters on the Half Shell
- Broiled Salt Roe Hering
- Boiled Rockfish
- Roast Beef and Yorkshire Pudding
- Mutton Chops
- Roast Suckling Pig
- Roast Turkey with Chestnut Stuffing
- Round of Cold Boiled Beef with Horse-radish Sauce
- Cold Baked Virginia Ham
- Lima Beans
- Baked Acorn Squash
- Baked Celery with Slivered Almonds
- Hominy Pudding
- Candied Sweet Potatoes
- Cantaloupe Pickle
- Spiced Peaches in Brandy
- Spiced Cranberries
- Mincemeat Pie
- Apple Pie
- Cherry Pie
- Chess Tarts
- Blancmange
- Plums in Wine Jelly
- Snowballs
- Indian Pudding
- Great Cake
- Ice Cream
- Plum Pudding
- Fruits
- Nuts
- Raisins
- Port
- Madeira

CHAPTER 2
ALEXANDER HAMILTON

Hip-Hop Hamilton

Why has government been instituted at all? Because the passions of man will not conform to the dictates of reason and justice without constraint.[10]

BORN: January 11, 1755 in Charlestown, Nevis, British West Indies

DIED: July 12, 1804 in New York City, New York

AGE AT DEATH: 49

CAUSE OF DEATH: He was shot and killed by Aaron Burr in a duel.

POLITICAL PARTY: Federalist Party

WIFE: Elizabeth Schuyler

CAREERS: United States secretary of the Treasury, founder of the Federalist Party, founder of the United States Revenue Cutter Service, which became the U.S. Coast Guard, founder of the *New York Post*, founder of the U.S. Mint

RELIGION: Presbyterian, converted to Episcopalian

NICKNAMES: Little Lion, Father of American Capitalism, Phocion (pseudonym), Publius (pseudonym), Caesar (a pseudonym used by Hamilton . . . maybe)

MEMORABLE QUOTE ABOUT HIM: "When America ceases to remember his greatness, America will no longer be great."—Calvin Coolidge[11]

FOUNDING DOCUMENTS SIGNED: The United States Constitution

BOOKS TO READ FOR MORE INFORMATION:
- *Alexander Hamilton* by Ron Chernow
- *Duel: Alexander Hamilton, Aaron Burr, and the Future of America* by Thomas Fleming
- *Alexander Hamilton: A Biography* by Forrest McDonald
- *The Intimate Life of Alexander Hamilton: Based Chiefly upon Original Family Letters and Other Documents, Many of Which Have Never Been Published* by Allan McLane Hamilton
- *Alexander Hamilton: Portrait in Paradox* by John C. Miller
- *Alexander Hamilton: Youth to Maturity, 1755-1788* by Broadus Mitchell
- *Alexander Hamilton: the Revolutionary Years* by Broadus Mitchell
- *Alexander Hamilton: America's Forgotten Founder* by Joseph A. Murray

Alexander Hamilton has always been a big deal in American history, but the attention has multiplied exponentially since the debut and enormous success of *Hamilton*, the musical.

The musical aside, why has Alexander Hamilton always been a subject of acclaim and interest in America? There were many reasons, not the least of which is that some historians believe America as we know it may not exist were it not for Hamilton's insight, vision, and wisdom.

The Alexander Hamilton Awareness Society has taken it upon itself to try to sum up "The Essence of Alexander Hamilton's Greatness"™ in 2 statements:

- **Alexander Hamilton**: George Washington's Indispensable Partner in War & Peace for over 22 Years
- **Alexander Hamilton**: Created the Vision & Foundation upon which the United States of America Achieved Greatness

That pretty much sums him up, wouldn't you say?

15 Things You Never Knew About Alexander Hamilton

17. Alexander Hamilton was born to an unwed couple on the island of Nevis in the Caribbean, and his father was a Scottish immigrant. His mother (who was married to someone else), was a Frenchwoman named

Rachel Fawcett Lavine from the British West Indies. In the *Hamilton* musical, the character of Aaron Burr describes Al as "a bastard, orphan, son of a whore and a Scotsman." (Yikes. Tell us you what you *really* think, Aaron . . .)

18. In order to score an apprenticeship, Hamilton told people he had been born in 1757. The truth? There's still argument, but he was likely born in 1755. We actually still don't know with certainty, though.

19. Hamilton was the founder of the U.S. Mint and the U.S. Coast Guard.

20. The naval communication book he wrote was still being used by America's Navy and Coast Guard during the Cuban Missile Crisis.

21. Hamilton founded what is today known as the *New York Post*. (You know the *Post*, right? Tabloid journalism at its best. Their most famous front page headline was "Headless Body in Topless Bar," which was written by Vincent Musetto, who died in June 2015.)

22. When Hamilton was 34, he embarked on an affair with a housewife named Maria Reynolds. Reynolds told Hamilton she was desperate for money, so their trysting turned very quickly into a "pay for play" entanglement. But not all was as it seemed: their liaison had been planned by Maria and her husband in order to blackmail and extort Hamilton. Hamilton paid, but in order to get out of another financial debacle, the husband claimed that Hamilton had paid his wife with government funds. During the investigation, Hamilton produced love letters from Maria and proof he had paid with his own money. The letters ended up in the hands of Hamilton's nemesis Thomas Jefferson, who promptly turned them over to a publisher who printed them in the newspaper.

23. In 1804, Alexander Hamilton was shot in a duel with then-Vice President Aaron Burr at Weehawken, New Jersey. The weapons were Wogdon pistols. He died shortly thereafter. (Yes, these gentlemen lived in a time when duels were accepted ways of settling disputes. Today, the only time a vice president shoots someone is by accident, right Dick Cheney?) Whether this historical note means anything or not, Hamilton's nineteen-year-old son Philip was also killed in a duel by a lawyer named George Eacker. Philip was infuriated by a highly critical speech Eacker gave about Alexander, his one and only dad, and when he confronted Eacker, he was challenged to a duel and agreed to it. Eacker didn't get a scratch on him. Philip, not so much. He died the next day.

Speaking words of wisdom . . .

Written by the sun

24. "The sacred rights of mankind are not to be rummaged for, among old parchments, or musty records. They are written, as with a sun beam, in the whole volume of human nature."[12]

Alexander Hamilton's dating profile

25. "Take her description—she must be young, handsome (I lay most stress upon a good shape), sensible (a little learning will do), well bred (but she must have an aversion to the word *ton*), chaste, and tender (I am an enthusiast in my notions of fidelity and fondness), of some good nature, for I dislike equally a termagant and an economist). In politics I am indifferent what side she may be of. I think I have arguments that will easily convert her to mine. As to religion a moderate stock will satisfy me. She must believe in God and hate a saint."[13]

What's that they say about absolute power . . . ?

26. "A fondness for power is implanted in most men, and it is natural to abuse it when acquired. This maxim, drawn from the experience of all ages, makes it the height of folly to intrust any set of men with power which is not under every possible control; perpetual strides are made after more as long as there is any part withheld."[14]

Trust, but verify . . .

27. "There may be in every government a few choice spirits, who may act from more worthy motives. One great error is that we suppose mankind more honest than they are. Our prevailing passions are ambition and interest."[15]

Impulsiveness can be dangerous . . .

28. "Has it not . . . invariably been found that momentary passions, and immediate interests, have a more active and imperious control over human conduct than general or remote considerations of policy, utility and justice?"[16]

Vanity? A vulnerability!

29. "Men are rather reasoning than reasonable animals for the most part governed by the impulse of passion. This is a truth well understood by our adversaries who have practised upon it with no small benefit to their cause. For at the very moment they are eulogizing the reason of men & professing to appeal only to that faculty, they are courting the strongest & most active passion of the human heart—VANITY!"[17]

Falsehoods mixed in . . .

30. "In all general questions which become the subjects of discussion, there are always some truths mixed with falsehoods. I confess, there is danger where men are capable of holding two offices. Take mankind in general, they are vicious, their passions may be operated upon. We have been taught to reprobate the danger of influence in the British government, without duly reflecting how far it was necessary to support a good government. We have taken up many ideas upon trust, and at last, pleased with our own opinions, establish them as undoubted truths."[18]

POTUS = CIC

31. "The President is to be commander-in-chief of the army and navy of the United States . . . It would amount to nothing more than the supreme command and direction of the military and naval forces, as first General and Admiral of the Confederacy; while that of the British king extends to the declaring of war and the raising and regulating of fleets and armies, — all of which by the Constitution under consideration, would appertain to the legislature."[19]

An Interview with Alexander Hamilton

Q: What do you think are the most important elements of an elected government?
A: Why has government been instituted at all? Because the passions of man will not conform to the dictates of reason and justice without constraint.

In framing a government which is to be administered by men over men, the great difficulty lies in this: you must first enable the government to control the governed; and in the next place, oblige it to control itself. Unless your government is respectable, foreigners will invade your rights; and to maintain tranquility, it must be respectable—even to observe neutrality, you must have a strong government. The honor of a nation is its life. A nation which can prefer disgrace to danger is prepared for a master, and deserves one.

Q: What are the most important things to keep in mind when drafting a Constitution?

A: Constitutions should consist only of general provisions; the reason is that they must necessarily be permanent, and that they cannot calculate for the possible change of things. It has been observed that a pure democracy if it were practicable would be the most perfect government. Experience has proved that no position is more false than this. The ancient democracies in which the people themselves deliberated never possessed one good feature of government. Their very character was tyranny; their figure deformity.

The origin of all civil government, justly established, must be a voluntary compact, between the rulers and the ruled; and must be liable to such limitations, as are necessary for the security of the absolute rights of the latter; for what original title can any man or set of men have, to govern others, except their own consent?

Q: If you don't mind my asking, sir, are you a Christian?

A: I have examined carefully the evidence of the Christian religion; and, if I was sitting as a juror upon its authenticity, I should unhesitatingly give my verdict in its favor. I have studied it, and I can prove its truth as clearly as any proposition ever submitted to the mind of man.

Q: What do you think about slavery?

A: Were not the disadvantages of slavery too obvious to stand in need of it, I might enumerate and describe the tedious train of calamities inseparable from it. I might show that it is fatal to religion and morality; that it tends to debase the mind, and corrupt its noblest springs of action. I might show that it relaxes the sinews of industry, clips the wings of commerce, and introduces misery and indigence in every shape.

Q: What are your thoughts about the 1 percent—that small percentage of Americans who control a huge amount of the country's wealth?

A: As riches increase and accumulate in few hands, as luxury prevails in society, virtue will be in a greater degree considered as only a graceful appendage of wealth, and the tendency of things will be to depart from the republican standard.

Q: How would you define liberty?

A: Liberty, according to my metaphysics is a self-determining power in an intellectual agent. It implies thought and choice and power.

Is the History in Hamilton for Reals?

Hamilton the musical shouldn't have happened. And if it did happen, it should not have been a roaring success.

Why? Because its triumph is a very rare instance of true originality being recognized and embraced—and succeeding financially. The arts in America are a tough business.

The pitch is absurd: "I want to do a hip-hop musical about Alexander Hamilton and cast the characters with no consideration for the race or gender of the actual historical figures." The response could have been something along the lines of, "Wait. What? A hip-hop history musical?"

For reals.

And Hamilton has beautifully fulfilled that hoary adage writers often use to try to sell their history tomes: "It makes history come alive!"

But how accurate are the multitude of historical details rapped about in the musical? Sure, it's based on a superb biography—Hamilton by Ron Chernow—but we all know what happens when one thing gets adapted into another thing. (Just ask any Stephen King fan.)

Some feel the musical doesn't paint an accurate (maybe "genuine" is a better word?) portrait of Hamilton. In the New York Times, David Waldstreicher of the Graduate Center of the City University of New York said, "The show, for all its redemptive and smart aspects, is part of this 'Founders Chic' phenomenon."[20]

Also in the Times, Annette Gordon-Reed, author of The Hemingses of Monticello, notes, "One of the most interesting things about the 'Hamilton' phenomenon is just how little serious criticism the play has received."

One element in particular which seems to have been easily accepted is the casting against type: being white or black, is irrelevant. A white actor plays a black man; a black man plays a white man. For instance, black actor Daveed Diggs portrays Thomas Jefferson. Aaron Burr, likewise, is played by a black actor.

But in an interview, Hamilton's creator and star Lin-Manuel Miranda responded bluntly when asked about the historical accuracy of the musical with, "Let's not pretend this is a textbook. Let's make the Founders of our country look like what our country looks like now."

But what about historical accuracy?

The portrayal of Alexander Hamilton is of what Princeton professor Sean Wilentz calls "an up-from-under hero," and that if Hamilton were around today he would be more "for the 1 percent than the 99 percent."

Hamilton is based on Ron Chernow's extraordinary biography Hamilton, and Chernow was the historical consultant for the musical. So it's got to be correct, right?

Factually, the musical seems to accurately depict the goings-on of the times. What people question is the reductionism in Miranda's interpretation of each character's views, sensibility, and words.

A valid response to that is, "Brother, please." This is a musical that runs two and half hours. Based on a book that runs 832 pages. Based on an American icon with decades of history to his name.

It's called "dramatic license."

And what is absolutely inspired about the musical is the casting. Usually, a movie or play will cast characters based on the author's depiction or the historical reality. But with the casting of *Hamilton*—blacks playing whites, etc.—the musical makes a subliminal and not-so-subliminal statement about Alexander Hamilton, the Founding Fathers, and the history of the United States.

It makes real something we fought a war for: the notion that all men are created equal.

Dig it.

BONUS – 14 Real Facts About the People & Times in Hamilton

- Ever hear of the Philolexian Society? No? That's not surprising since it was a top secret literary and debate society that was founded by Alexander Hamilton and other select students when he attended Columbia University. It is still in existence to this day.
- Aaron Burr was only 36 when he was offered a seat on the New York Supreme Court in 1792. He turned it down.
- Behind closed doors, who knows what went on, but in Alexander Hamilton's time, married women were required to unquestioningly obey their husband.
- This had to hurt: When Aaron Burr's second wife Eliza filed for divorce because she believed he was stealing from her, her lawyer was his nemesis Alexander Hamilton's son, Alexander Hamilton II.
- James Madison was one of the first men of Hamilton's time to wear pants. Breeches had been the go-to style for men prior to that.
- Alexander Hamilton's sister-in-law Angelica and the Marquis De Lafayette were pen pals.
- And you thought chicken soup was the way to go, right? When Alexander Hamilton's sister-in-law Peggy Schuyler was sick, Ham brought her a basket of crabs.
- The quality of accessible water was so bad in Hamilton's time that many farmers would give their cows beer. The resultant milk was disgusting and disease-laden.
- Thomas Jefferson's daughter, Maria, went to school with Hamilton's sister-in-law Angelica's daughter, Kitty. The two girls remained lifelong friends.
- If you could afford a carriage drawn by 4 horses in Hamilton's time, people perceived you as pretty well off.
- Eliza Hamilton established the first private orphanage in New York. It is still in existence and is now called Graham Windham. The cast of *Hamilton* has performed there and raised money for the institution.
- *Hamilton*'s popularity persuaded the United States Treasury to forgo their plans to replace Alexander Hamilton on the front of the $10 bill.
- *Hamilton* can be credited with achieving what many thought was an impossible task: Young people who are fans of the musical have become interested in U.S. colonial history and the people who founded America.
- Benjamin Franklin was cut completely from the musical. He had one song, "Diplomacy Happens At Night," but it didn't make the final cut.

CHAPTER 3
THOMAS JEFFERSON

Man of the Mind

When angry count to ten before you speak. If very angry, count to one hundred.[21]

BORN: April 13, 1743 in Shadwell, Virginia

DIED: July 4, 1826 in Charlottesville, Virginia

AGE AT DEATH: 83

CAUSE OF DEATH: According to www.Monticello. org, Jefferson's likely cause of death was "exhaustion from intense diarrhea, toxemia from a kidney infection, uremia from kidney damage, and finally orthostatic old-age pneumonia" as well as possibly undiagnosed prostate cancer.[22]

POLITICAL PARTY: Democratic-Republican

FIRST LADY: Martha Wayles Skelton

CAREERS: Third president of the United States, secretary of state, minister to France, governor of Virginia, Second Continental Congress delegate, founder of University of Virginia, lawyer

RELIGION: Deist

NICKNAMES: Father of the Declaration of Independence, Long Tom, the Pen of the Revolution, the Philosopher of Democracy, the Sage of Monticello, Man of the People

MEMORABLE QUOTE ABOUT HIM: "He was certainly one of the most learned men of the age. It may be said of him as has been said of others that he was a 'walking Library,' and what can be said of but few such prodigies, that the Genius of Philosophy ever walked hand in hand with him."—James Madison[23]

FOUNDING DOCUMENT SIGNED: The Declaration of Independence[24]

BOOKS TO READ FOR MORE INFORMATION:

- *Twilight at Monticello: The Final Years of Thomas Jefferson* by Alan Pell Crawford
- *American Sphinx* by Joseph J. Ellis
- *The Hemingses of Monticello* by Annette Gordon-Reed
- *Jefferson and His Time* by Dumas Malone
- *The Jefferson Image in the American Mind* by Merrill D. Peterson

One wonders what it must have been like to live with Thomas Jefferson. There's a funny scene in an episode of The West Wing in which First Lady Abigail Bartlet offers a bit of romantic advice to the daughter of a friend: "Don't go for the geniuses," she advises. "They never want to sleep."

Can we even begin to imagine what Thomas Jefferson would have written and accomplished if he lived in our time? We look at what he achieved writing by hand and without electricity and are awed by the manifestation of his genius in what he left behind, his legacy. Thomas Jefferson with a computer? Boggle, the mind does.

Jefferson was the 3rd president of the United States, the 2nd vice president, the principal author of the Declaration of Independence (at the young age of 33), the United States minister to France, America's first secretary of state, a planter, surveyor, landowner, inventor, and, of course, slaveholder. He acquired the Louisiana Territory from Napoleon, he moved Native Americans (whether they wanted to be moved or not) to the new Louisiana Territory, and had problems with the Barbary pirates.

He and his wife Martha had 6 children, and his legacy is that of a polymath genius with extraordinary vision.

23 Things You Never Knew About Thomas Jefferson

32. Do you like French fries? You have Thomas Jefferson to thank since he was the one who, after a trip to France during which he enjoyed *pommes frites*, introduced to America the delight of the fried potato.

33. Jefferson sold 10,000 books to the U.S. government to restart the Library of Congress after the British burned it down in 1814.

34. Are you at work? Are you seated at a desk? Are you sitting on a swivel chair? Thomas Jefferson invented it. (The swivel chair, not the desk.)

35. When Thomas Jefferson edited the Bible by removing all the supernatural stuff—and that's not an overstatement: he took out anything and everything that purported a violation of Natural Law—he put it away and left specific instructions that it not be made public or published until seventy-five years after his death. He knew better.

36. On Thomas Jefferson's tombstone is the following:

HERE WAS BURIED
THOMAS JEFFERSON
AUTHOR OF THE
DECLARATION
OF
AMERICAN INDEPENDENCE
OF THE STATUTE OF VIRGINIA
FOR
RELIGIOUS FREEDOM
AND FATHER OF THE
UNIVERSITY OF VIRGINIA

He left specific instructions before his death as to what to inscribe: " . . . on the faces of the Obelisk the following inscription, & not a word more because by these, as testimonials that I have lived, I wish most to be remembered." Note what's missing. His term as president of the United States.

37. Jefferson's inauguration was the first held in Washington, D. C.

38. Jefferson walked to his inauguration. He wore a plain gray suit, and many long believed it was because he wanted to show he was just an ordinary man. The truth, as it often is, is a tad trickier: Jefferson had a velvet suit handmade for his inauguration, as well as a very expensive carriage in which to ride. Neither were ready the day of the inauguration, so he walked.

39. Jefferson's last words were "Is it the Fourth?" (It was.)

40. Thomas Jefferson was only 33 years old when he wrote "We hold these truths to be self-evident, that all men are created equal . . ."

41. Jefferson was a contradiction. He once said that if he had to choose between a government without newspapers or newspapers without

government, he would choose newspapers. But he also wanted the state to sue for libel newspapers who didn't like him or his presidency. Not very "First Amendmenty" there, eh, Tom?

42. In Thomas Jefferson's will, he left "my gold mounted walking staff of animal horn as a token of cordial and affectionate friendship" to James Madison.

43. In his first draft of the Declaration of Independence, Thomas Jefferson referred to slavery as "the execrable commerce." The gents of the Continental Congress did not like that term and cut it. Jefferson was . . . well, "displeased" would be a polite way of putting it.

Speaking words of wisdom . . .

Jefferson believed in the gold standard . . .

44. An 1884 essay by George Bancroft titled "A Plea for the Constitution of the United States" includes this opinion from Thomas Jefferson: "The federal government—I deny their power to make paper money a legal tender."

TJ, too, was obviously tired of religion . . .

45. "I contemplate with sovereign reverence that act of the whole American people which declared that their legislature should make no law respecting an establishment of religion, or prohibit the free exercise thereof, thus building a wall of separation between church and state." [25]

Here's that "Wall" quote that drives everybody crazy . . .

46. "Because religious belief, or non-belief, is such an important part of every person's life, freedom of religion affects every individual. State churches that use government power to support themselves and force their views on persons of other faiths undermine all our civil rights. Moreover, state support of the church tends to make the clergy unresponsive to the people and leads to corruption within religion. Erecting the "wall of separation between church and state," therefore, is absolutely essential in a free society. We have solved . . . the great and interesting question whether freedom of religion is compatible with order in government and obedience to the laws. And we have experienced the quiet as well as the comfort which results from leaving every one to profess freely and openly

those principles of religion which are the inductions of his own reason and the serious convictions of his own inquiries."[26]

Quarreling, fighting, burning, and torturing . . . over religion . . .

47. "On the dogmas of religion, as distinguished from moral principles, all mankind, from the beginning of the world to this day, have been quarreling, fighting, burning and torturing one another, for abstractions unintelligible to themselves and to all others, and absolutely beyond the comprehension of the human mind. Were I to enter that arena, I should only add an unit to the number of Bedlamites."[27]

The truth doesn't need priests . . .

48. "In every country and in every age, the priest has been hostile to liberty. He is always in alliance with the despot, abetting his abuses in return for protection to his own. It is error alone that needs the support of government. Truth can stand by itself." [28]

Christians hate these quotes . . .

49. "It is too late in the day for men of sincerity to pretend they believe in the Platonic mysticisms that 3 are 1, and 1 is 3; and yet that the 1 is not 3, and the 3 are not 1 But this constitutes the craft, the power and the profit of the priests. Sweep away their gossamer fabrics of factitious religion, and they would catch no more flies. We should all then, like the Quakers, live without an order of priests, moralize for ourselves, follow the oracle of conscience, and say nothing about what no man can understand, nor therefore believe."[29]

50. "The priests have so disfigured the simple religion of Jesus that no one who reads the sophistications they have engrafted on it, from the jargon of Plato, of Aristotle and other mystics, would conceive these could have been fathered on the sublime preacher of the Sermon on the Mount. Yet, knowing the importance of names, they have assumed that of Christians, while they are mere Platonists, or anything rather than disciples of Jesus."[30]

51. "Altho' I rarely waste time in reading on theological subjects, as mangled by our Pseudo-Christians, yet I can readily suppose Basanistos may be amusing. Ridicule is the only weapon which can be used against unintelligible propositions. Ideas must be distinct before reason can act

upon them; and no man ever had a distinct idea of the trinity. It is mere Abracadabra of the mountebanks calling themselves the priests of Jesus. If it could be understood it would not answer their purpose. Their security is in their faculty of shedding darkness, like the scuttlefish, thro' the element in which they move, and making it impenetrable to the eye of a pursuing enemy, and there they will skulk.[31]

52. "Question with boldness even the existence of a God; because, if there be one, he must more approve of the homage of reason, then that of blindfolded fear."[32]

Let the NSA try and beat that!

53. "[I have] an opportunity of sending you a cipher to be used between us, which will give you some trouble to understand, but, once understood, is the easiest to use, the most indecipherable, and varied by a new key with the greatest facility of any one I have ever known. I am in hopes the explanation inclosed will be sufficient. [It is] produced by writing our names and residences at full length, each of which containing 27 letters is divided into two parts of 9 letters each; and each of the 9 letters is then numbered according to the place it would hold if the 9 were arranged alphabetically . . . The numbers over the letters being then arranged as the letters to which they belong stand in our names, we can always construct our key."[33]

The dog of war . . .

54. "We have already given in example one effectual check to the dog of war by transferring the power of letting him loose from the Executive to the Legislative body."[34]

THE ONE THING

The Founders were men of scholarship. They read widely, had impressive vocabularies, learned languages, studied mathematics, invented things, and devoted a great deal of their time to personal growth and achievement.

And remember that we're talking about them achieving these things during a time when learning was a chore. Books were expensive and difficult to acquire. Correspondence took ages; writing was done in longhand.

Yet they all persevered to learn more and to be the best at whatever they were doing.

Since then, many things have changed, some of which are touched on in the Introduction. We cannot help but wonder what the Founders would have achieved if they had had access to . . . well, everything we have access to today.

This spurs the question: If any of the Founders were magically transported to our time, what would be the one thing that would amaze them the most?

I've asked this question of teachers, researchers, scholars, and everyday people, and the consensus seems to be that they would have been most amazed by the reality that anyone can have access to all the knowledge that exists via a small device that can fit in a pocket.

This, the teeming masses agree, would have blown them away.

The smartphone (and, by extension, the Internet) would have been the realization and manifestation for them of a dream come true: easy, inexpensive, fast access to knowledge.

Of course there would be countless other developments that would mesmerize them: planes, cars, the phone, fast food, supermarkets, indoor plumbing, the flush toilet, department stores, TV, microwaves, refrigerators, elevators, search engines, the remote control, printers, air conditioning . . . the list does, indeed, go on and on.

But knowing what we know about the Founders, they'd *get it*. Immediately. Google and Wikipedia are simply extensions of a concept they fully understood: information storage and retrieval. Only the Founders had to use books.

The One Thing: the smartphone.

What would these icons have done with *that*?

An Interview with Thomas Jefferson

Q: Thank you for taking the time to talk with us today, Mr. President. I see you've been spending some time in your garden lately.

A: No occupation is so delightful to me as the culture of the earth, and no culture comparable to that of the garden . . . But though an old man, I am but a young gardener.

Cultivators of the earth are the most valuable citizens. They are the most vigorous, the most independent, the most virtuous, and they are tied to their country and wedded to its liberty and interests by the most lasting bands. As long therefore as they can find employment in this line, I would not convert them into mariners, artisans, or any thing else. But our citizens will find employment in this line till their numbers, and of course their productions, become too great for the demand both internal and foreign.

Q: You recently spent quite a lot of time working on the Declaration of Independence and the Constitution. What kind of future do you see for Americans?

A: I predict future happiness for Americans, if they can prevent the government from wasting the labors of the people under the pretense of taking care of them.

Q: You have quite a library, but I don't see any newspapers around. Is it true you're not a fan of that particular forum?

A: The man who reads nothing at all is better educated than the man who reads nothing but newspapers. The people cannot be all, and always, well informed. The part which is wrong will be discontented, in proportion to the importance of the facts they misconceive. If they remain quiet under such misconceptions, it is lethargy, the forerunner of death to the public liberty.

Q: What do you think about the increasing power of corporations in our country?

A. I hope that we shall crush in its birth the aristocracy of our monied corporations, which dare already to challenge our government to a trial of strength, and bid defiance to the laws of our country.

Q: How would you describe, Mr. President, the American way of government to a curious foreigner?

A: We think in America that it is necessary to introduce the people into every department of government as far as they are capable of exercising it; and that this is the only way to ensure a long-continued and honest administration of its powers.

1. They are not qualified to exercise themselves the *Executive* department: but they are qualified to name the person who shall exercise it. With us therefore they choose this officer every four years.
2. They are not qualified to *legislate*. With us therefore they only choose the legislators.
3. They are not qualified to *judge* questions of law; but they are very capable of judging questions of fact. In the form of *juries* therefore they determine all matters of fact, leaving to the permanent judges to decide the law resulting from those facts.

   But we all know that permanent judges acquire an esprit de corps; that, being known, they are liable to be tempted by bribery; that they are misled by favor, by relationship, by a spirit of party, by a devotion to the executive or legislative; that it is better to leave a cause to the decision of cross and pile than to that of a judge biased to one side; and that the opinion of twelve honest jurymen gives still a better hope of right than cross and pile does.

   It is left therefore, to the juries, if they think the permanent judges are under any bias whatever in any cause, to take on themselves to judge the law as well as the fact. They never exercise this power but when they suspect partiality in the judges; and by the exercise of this power they have been the firmest bulwarks of English liberty.

Q: You, sir, are multilingual. Why is it important to speak more than one language?

A: With respect to modern languages, French, as I have before observed, is indispensable. Next to this the Spanish is most important to an American. Our connection with Spain is already important and will become daily more so. Besides this the ancient part of American history is written chiefly in Spanish.

CHAPTER 4
JOHN ADAMS

The Tea Partier

Democracy . . . while it lasts is more bloody than either aristocracy or monarchy. Remember, democracy never lasts long. It soon wastes, exhausts, and murders itself. There is never a democracy that did not commit suicide.[35]

BORN: October 30, 1735 in Braintree, Massachusetts

DIED: July 4, 1826 in Quincy, Massachusetts

AGE AT DEATH: 90

CAUSE OF DEATH: Heart failure and pneumonia. Adams's death culminated a period of deterioration that confined him to his home and prevented him from attending the celebration marking the fiftieth anniversary of the creation of the United States.[36]

POLITICAL PARTY: Federalist Party

FIRST LADY: Abigail Smith

CAREERS: Second president of the United States, delegate to the First Continental Congress, delegate to the Second Continental Congress, lawyer, author, diplomat

RELIGION: Unitarian

NICKNAMES: Atlas of Independence, the Colossus of American Independence, the Duke of Braintree, His Rotundity

John Adams was born in Quincy, Massachusetts. His father was a farmer and a deacon, and he excelled educationally, graduating from Harvard with a master's degree in 1755. He got into politics in his 30s, mainly because he was angry abut the Stamp Act, the British law that taxed colonists for, essentially, every piece of paper they generated and used.

As a lawyer he got 6 of the British soldiers involved in the Boston Massacre acquitted, and he represented Massachusetts at the First Continental Convention. (People hated him for this, by the way, and his law practice suffered as a result.)

He spent 10 years in Europe negotiating treaties and ultimately became George Washington's vice president, followed by being elected president himself in 1796.

Adams and his wife Abigail had 6 children, and his son John Quincy Adams would be elected the 6th president of the United States.

19 Things You Never Knew About John Adams

55. Thomas Jefferson once described John Adams as "vain" and "irritable."
56. John Adams believed that America's Independence Day would be July 2nd. In a letter to his wife, he wrote, "The Second Day of July 1776, will be the most memorable Epocha, in the History of America."[38] (Interestingly, this was the day the Signers held a booze-soaked party. They signed two days later. See the "Drink Up! The Alcoholic Beverages Consumed Two Days Before the Signing of the Declaration of Independence" in *The Reading Room* section of this book)
57. John Adams started smoking at the age of 8.

58. John Adams had a serious lisp. Historians believe it's because he had no teeth.

59. John Adams, a Unitarian, wouldn't work on Sundays during the Revolutionary War. This policy was ultimately tossed when he was president. It probably had something to do with that oath he swore about "preserving and protecting the Constitution" in 1797. Not a nine-to-five, Monday through Friday job by any means.

60. One of Adams's biggest missteps as president was signing the Alien and Sedition Acts in 1798. These laws essentially gave the government the power to deport any alien they didn't like. That's a flip way of describing its powers, but it's accurate. You're an alien from Spain and the U.S. goes to war with Spain? You're gone. You say nasty things about the president? You're outta here. Someone hints to someone in power that you *could* be a danger to America? Buh-bye. In 1802, Congress repealed one of the acts, the Naturalization Act, and all the other laws of the Acts were allowed to expire. Today, Constitutional scholars are almost unanimous in their agreement that the Alien and Sedition Acts were unconstitutional.

61. John Adams never owned a single slave. Yet he was anti-abolition. Why? Because he felt that eliminating the institution of slavery would cause turmoil and destabilization and bring the ruckus to the new nation.

62. On a trip from Philadelphia to New York, John Adams and Benjamin Franklin shared a bed. No room at the inn, apparently.

63. Adams ran for president against Thomas Jefferson and beat him by three votes. Adams ended up a 1-term president, however, when Jefferson got his revenge by beating Adams the second time he ran against him.

Speaking Words of Wisdom . . .

64. "Thomas Jefferson still survives."[39]
65. "The government of the United States is not, in any sense, founded on the Christian religion."[40]

Innocent until proven . . .

66. "It is more important that innocence be protected than it is that guilt be punished, for guilt and crimes are so frequent in this world that they cannot all be punished. But if innocence itself is brought to the bar and condemned, perhaps to die, then the citizen will say, 'whether I do good

or whether I do evil is immaterial, for innocence itself is no protection,' and if such an idea as that were to take hold in the mind of the citizen that would be the end of security whatsoever."[41]

67. "It is more important that innocence be protected than it is that guilt be punished, for guilt and crimes are so frequent in this world that they cannot all be punished. But if innocence itself is brought to the bar and condemned, perhaps to die, then the citizen will say, 'whether I do good or whether I do evil is immaterial, for innocence itself is no protection,' and if such an idea as that were to take hold in the mind of the citizen that would be the end of security whatsoever."[42]

68. "Facts are stubborn things; and whatever may be our wishes, our inclinations, or the dictates of our passion, they cannot alter the state of facts and evidence."[43]

There's hope for us all yet . . .

69. "We should begin by setting conscience free. When all men of all religions shall enjoy equal liberty, property, and an equal chance for honors and power we may expect that improvements will be made in the human character and the state of society." [44]

Liberty . . .

70. "But a Constitution of Government once changed from Freedom, can never be restored, Liberty, once lost, is lost forever."[45]

71. "Liberty, according to my metaphysics is a self-determining power in an intellectual agent. It implies thought and choice and power."[46]

72. "The jaws of power are always open to devour, and her arm is always stretched out, if possible, to destroy the freedom of thinking, speaking, and writing."[47]

A Dog Named Satan (Nope, wasn't a Pit!)

John and Abigail Adams had a mixed breed dog named Satan. (That name prompts the question: Did they have obedience lessons for dogs back then?) They also had another dog named Juno and a horse named Cleopatra.

It don't come easy . . .

73. "I am well aware of the toil, and blood, and treasure, that it will cost us to maintain this declaration, and support and defend these states. Yet, through all the gloom, I can see the rays of light and glory; I can see that the end is more than worth all the means, and that posterity will triumph, although you and I may rue, which I hope we shall not."[48]

An Interview with John Adams

Q: **What elements do you think should be included in a perfect educational system?**

A: I must study politics and war that my sons may have liberty to study mathematics and philosophy. My sons ought to study mathematics and philosophy, geography, natural history, naval architecture, navigation, commerce, and agriculture, in order to give their children a right to study painting, poetry, music, architecture, statuary, tapestry, and porcelain. Liberty cannot be preserved without general knowledge among the people. Let us tenderly and kindly cherish, therefore, the means of knowledge. Let us dare to read, think, speak, and write.

Q: **What are your thoughts about being vice president?**

A: My country has contrived for me the most insignificant office that ever the invention of man contrived or his imagination conceived.

Q: **Do you have any thoughts on the American Revolution and the birth and establishment of the United States?**

A: But what do we mean by the American Revolution? Do we mean the American war? The Revolution was effected before the war commenced. The Revolution was in the minds and hearts of the people; a change in their religious sentiments, of their duties and obligations . . . This radical change in the principles, opinions, sentiments, and affections of the people was the real American Revolution.

I always consider the settlement of America with reverence and wonder, as the opening of a grand scene and design in providence, for the illumination of the ignorant and the emancipation of the slavish part of mankind all over the earth. [But] the Declaration of Independence I always considered as a theatrical show. Jefferson ran away with all the stage effect of that . . . and all the glory of it.

Q: **I'm sure you're aware, Mr. President, that people hate paying taxes. What are your thoughts on taxation?**

A: Each individual of the society has a right to be protected by it in the enjoyment of his life, liberty, and property, according to standing laws. He is obliged, consequently, to contribute his share to the expense of this protection; and to give his personal service, or an equivalent, when necessary. But no part of the property of any individual can, with justice, be taken from him, or applied to public uses, without his own consent, or that of the representative body of the people. In fine, the people of this commonwealth are not controllable by any other laws than those to which their constitutional representative body have given their consent.

Q: **What are your guiding principles, Mr. President, regarding the actual idea of "government." We don't have a king; we have elected officials whom the people put into office. Is this ultimately a good system?**

A: Government is instituted for the common good; for the protection, safety, prosperity, and happiness of the people; and not for profit, honor, or private interest of any one man, family, or class of men; therefore, the people alone have an incontestable, unalienable, and indefeasible right to institute government; and to reform, alter, or totally change the same, when their protection, safety, prosperity, and happiness require it.

CHAPTER 5
BENJAMIN FRANKLIN

Dude Was Wired Up

Early to be and early to rise, makes a man healthy, wealthy, and wise.[49]

From a child I was fond of reading, and all the little money that came into my hands was ever laid out in books.[50]

BORN: January 17, 1706 in Boston, Massachusetts

DIED: April 17, 1790 in Philadelphia, Pennsylvania

AGE AT DEATH: 84

CAUSE OF DEATH: Pleurisy. Franklin also had emphysema and a high fever, and his lungs were filled with pus. Prior to his death, he was bedridden and in great pain, ameliorated only by morphine. Franklin himself had designed the black-bordered edition of the *Pennsylvania Gazette* that would announce his death.

POLITICAL PARTY: Independent

WIFE: Deborah Read

CAREERS: President of Pennsylvania, U.S. minister to Sweden and France, 1st U.S. postmaster general, inventor

RELIGION: Raised Episcopalian, later became a Deist

NICKNAMES & PSEUDONYMS: Water American, Poor Richard, The First American, Silence Dogood, The Newton of Electricity, The Prophet of Tolerance, The Patron Saint of Advertising, Anthony Afterwit, Polly Baker, Alice Addertongue, Caelia Shortface, Martha Careful, Busy Body, Benevolous

MEMORABLE QUOTE ABOUT HIM: "Dr. Franklin is well known to be the greatest philosopher of the present age;— all the operations of nature he seems to understand,—the very heavens obey him, and the Clouds yield up their Lightning to be imprisoned in his rod."—William Pierce[51]

FOUNDING DOCUMENTS SIGNED: The Declaration of Independence, the Treaty of Paris[52], the United States Constitution

BOOKS TO READ FOR MORE INFORMATION:
* *The Autobiography of Benjamin Franklin*
* *Benjamin Franklin: An American Life* by Walter Isaacson
* *The Life of Benjamin Franklin* (3 vols.) by J. A. Leo Lemay
* *The Americanization of Benjamin Franklin* by Gordon Wood
* *Benjamin Franklin* by Carl Van Doren

Benjamin Franklin helped draft the Declaration of Independence and the United States Constitution but there was much more to him than politics. Due to his failing health, Franklin needed assistance to sign the United States Constitution. Reportedly, tears streamed down his face as he did so.

He was a member of the team that negotiated the treaty that ended the Revolutionary War, he wrote *Poor Richard's Almanack*, and was one of fifteen children born to a candle maker named Josiah Franklin. He was also an inventor, printer, newspaper owner, and slaveholder.

He invented a musical instrument and came up with a new alphabet that eliminated the letters C, J, Q, W, X, and Y. He believed they were superfluous and that we could survive quite nicely without them.

He was on the Philadelphia City Council, he was a member of the Pennsylvania Assembly, and he testified against the Stamp Act before Parliament.

He suffered from gout all his life and died from an array of complications, with pleurisy being a particularly egregious one.

Franklin died in 1790. He had written his own epitaph when he was 22:

The body of B. Franklin, Printer (Like the Cover of an Old Book Its Contents torn Out And Stript of its Lettering and Gilding) Lies Here, Food for Worms. But the Work shall not be Lost; For it will (as he Believ'd) Appear once More In a New and More Elegant Edition Revised and Corrected By the Author."

His family didn't use it. On his gravestone reads,"Benjamin and Deborah Franklin 1790."

27 Things You Never Knew About Benjamin Franklin

74. Are you nearsighted? Farsighted? Wear bifocals? Thank Benjamin Franklin. He invented them.

75. Have urinary troubles? Use a flexible catheter? Thank Benjamin Franklin. He invented it.

76. Benjamin Franklin became a wealthy man, but not from his inventions. He made a lot of money from *Poor Richard's Almanack* and his newspaper, *The Pennsylvania Gazette*.

77. When Benjamin Franklin was 17, he proposed to Deborah Read, who was 15. Read's mother refused to allow the marriage. Seven years later, Franklin and Read entered into a common-law marriage and raised Franklin's illegitimate son William.

78. In an April 25, 1784, letter to Benjamin Webb, a man who owed him money, Franklin talked about a practice that had been around for a long time, but became popular due to Franklin, and it's still popular today. That practice is called "Pay It Forward":

> When you [. . .] meet with another honest Man in similar Distress, you must pay me by lending this Sum to him; enjoining him to discharge the Debt by a like operation, when he shall be able, and shall meet with another opportunity. I hope it may thus go thro' many hands, before it meets with a Knave that will stop its Progress. This is a trick of mine for doing a deal of good with a little money.

79. Benjamin Franklin discovered that pouring oil overboard when at sea steadied the ship. This technique was used in 1912 to settle the *Carpathia* as it picked up survivors from the *Titanic* sinking.

80. Benjamin Franklin loved chess. In December 1786, he wrote an essay called "The Morals of Chess," which was published in *Columbian* magazine. It was the second known piece of writing in America about chess. The essay included this line, "The Games of Chess is not merely an idle amusement; several very valuable qualities of the mind, useful in the course of human life, are to be acquired and strengthened by it, so as to become habits ready on all occasions." The first writing about chess in America was a poem by Rev. Lewis Rou in 1744 about New York chess players.[53]

81. For 4½, there was a state called Franklin, named for Benjamin Franklin. It was never admitted into the Union. It was in what is now eastern Tennessee.

82. Benjamin Franklin had 16 brothers and sisters, 7 of whom were from his father's 1st marriage.

83. Benjamin Franklin's formal education stopped when he was 10 years old.

84. At one point during his life Benjamin Franklin had a bladder stone that grew so large, they couldn't operate to remove it, and there was nothing else that could be done for it. BF used opium to dull the pain the stone caused.

85. Franklin knew from an early age that anyone who could write well in the eighteenth century would garner a great deal of attention, so he set out to become an excellent prose writer. He trained himself by voracious reading, and copying by hand essays from books and magazines. He wrote in his *Autobiography* that prose writing became "of great Use to me in the Course of my Life, and was a principal Means of my Advancement."[54.]

86. When Benjamin Franklin was 17, he wrote a series of satirical essays about a wide range of topics pertinent to the times, and used the byline of "Silence Dogood." That's right: an 18-year-old boy took on the persona of a cantankerous middle-aged woman—and quite successfully, too. It please Franklin greatly that even his own brothers couldn't deduce that Mrs. Dogood was their younger brother.

87. Benjamin Franklin went to London when he was eighteen to work as a printer. While there, he wrote an essay called "A Dissertation on Liberty and Necessity, Pleasure and Pain." In it, he took the position that man did not really have free will because everything that happened was due to an omnipotent God, and therefore he could not be held morally responsible for his actions. Today, it is believed he wrote it because he felt guilty about being a party guy in London and indulging himself in all manner of delights. He later repudiated the essay and only 1 copy survived. It's all over the Internet now, though.

88. Franklin's interest in electricity, undertaken after he retired to live as a wealthy "gentleman" at the age of 42, resulted in him coining new words still used today, including *conductor, charge, discharge, condense, armature, electrify,* and several others.

89. At the end of his long life, as Benjamin Franklin was failing, his daughter made him shift his position on the bed to help his breathing. We really don't know if this killed him or not, but we do know his last words were, "A dying man can do nothing easy."

90. Is lightning divine? After Benjamin Franklin invented the lightning rod, some of the oh-so-pious religious leaders of the time thought it was evil and should not be used. Why? Because with it, Franklin was trying to control a divine power. Fortunately, not many people of the time listened to the holy men, and countless houses were saved from the flames tanks to Franklin's "evil" invention.

91. Two-thirds of the population of Philadelphia—20,000 people—attended Benjamin Franklin's funeral.

Speaking words of wisdom . . .

Poor Richard speaks . . .

92. "Three may keep a secret, if two of them are dead."[55]

93. "Never confuse Motion with Action."[56]

94. "Be at war with your vices, at peace with your neighbors, and let every new year find you a better man."[57]

95. "An investment in knowledge pays the best interest."[58]

96. "Whoever would overthrow the liberty of a nation must begin by subduing the freeness of speech."[59]

How to tell a good religion from a bad one . . .

97. "When a religion is good, I conceive it will support itself; and when it does not support itself, and God does not take care to support it so that its professors are obligated to call for help of the civil power, it's a sign, I apprehend, of its being a bad one."[60]

98. "If we look back into history for the character of present sects in Christianity, we shall find few that have not in their turns been persecutors, and complainers of persecution. The primitive Christians thought persecution extremely wrong in the Pagans, but practised it on one another. The first Protestants of the Church of England, blamed persecution in the Roman church, but practised it against the Puritans: these found it wrong in the Bishops, but fell into the same practice themselves both here and in New England."[61]

There has been a great deal of discussion regarding the item "address *Powerful Goodness*." What was Franklin referring to? Since Franklin was a Deist for most of his adult life, a logical conclusion can be that Franklin spent this time contemplatively and meditating on a higher power or a greater good.

Flawed government is better than no government . . .

100. "I agree to this Constitution with all its faults, if they are such: because I think a General Government necessary for us, and there is no Form of Government but what may be a Blessing to the People if well-administered; and I believe farther that this is likely to be well administered for a Course of Years and can only end in Despotism as other Forms have done before it, when the People shall become so corrupted as to need Despotic Government, being incapable of any other."[62]

What would Ben think of today's op-eds?

101. "The Conductor of a Newspaper, should, methinks, consider himself as in some degree the Guardian of his Country's Reputation, and refuse to insert such Writings as may hurt it. If People will print their Abuses of one another, let them do it in little Pamphlets, and distribute them where they think proper. It is absurd to trouble all the World with them; and unjust to Subscribers in distant Places, to stuff their Papers with Matters so unprofitable & so disagreable."[63]

An Interview with Benjamin Franklin

Q: **What advice would you offer young people today?**

A: Many people die at 25 and aren't buried until they are 75. The Constitution only guarantees the American people the right to pursue happiness. You have to catch it yourself. Work as if you were to live 1,000 years, play as if you were to die tomorrow. If you fail to plan, you are planning to fail! You can do anything you set your mind to, and there will be sleeping enough in the grave.

Sloth makes all things difficult, but industry all easy; and he that rises late must trot all day, and shall scarce overtake his business at night; while laziness travels so slowly, that poverty soon overtakes him.

All highly competent people continually search for ways to keep learning, growing, and improving. They do that by asking WHY? After all, the person who knows HOW will always have a job, but the person who knows WHY? will always be the boss. Be studious in your profession, and you will be learned. Be industrious and frugal, and you will be rich. Be sober and temperate, and you will be healthy. Be in general virtuous, and you will be happy. At least you will, by such conduct, stand the best chance for such consequences.

Q: **What do you think about safety nets? Welfare, unemployment, food stamps, and so forth?**

A: I am for doing good to the poor, but I think the best way of doing good to the poor, is not making them easy in poverty, but leading or driving them out of it. I observed that the more public provisions were made for the poor, the less they provided for themselves, and of course became poorer. And, on the contrary, the less was done for them, the more they did for themselves, and became richer. When the people find that they can vote themselves money that will herald the end of the republic.

Q: **Mark Twain once said that there is no difference between the man who can't read and the man who doesn't read.**

A: The person who deserves most pity is a lonesome one on a rainy day who doesn't know how to read. Genius without education is like silver in the mine. All the little money that ever came into my hands was ever laid out in books.

Q: **What do you think about slavery?**

A: Slavery is such an atrocious debasement of human nature, that its very extirpation, if not performed with solicitous care, may sometimes open a source of serious evils. The unhappy man who has been treated as a brute animal, too frequently sinks beneath the common standard of the human species. The galling chains, that bind his body, do also fetter his intellectual faculties, and impair the social affections of his heart . . . To instruct, to advise, to qualify those, who have been restored to freedom, for the exercise and enjoyment of civil liberty . . . and to procure for their children an education calculated for their future situation in life; these are the great outlines of the annexed plan, which we have adopted.

Q: How would you describe or define happiness?

A: Happiness consists more in the small conveniences of pleasures that occur every day, than in great pieces of good fortune that happen but seldom to a man in the course of his life.

Q: What are your feelings about religion? Do you "subscribe," so to speak, to one particular denomination?

A: You desire to know something of my Religion. It is the first time I have been questioned upon it: But I do not take your Curiosity amiss, and shall endeavour in a few Words to gratify it . . . I have, with most of the present Dissenters in England, some Doubts as to his [Jesus'] divinity; tho' it is a question I do not dogmatize upon, having never studied it, and I think it needless to busy myself with it now, when I expect soon an Opportunity of knowing the Truth with less Trouble.

My Parents had early given me religious Impressions, and brought me through my Childhood piously in the Dissenting Way. But I was scarce 15 when, after doubting by turns of several Points as I found them disputed in the different Books I read, I began to doubt of Revelation itself. Some Books against Deism fell into my Hands; they were said to be the Substance of Sermons preached at Boyle's Lectures. It happened that they wrought an Effect on me quite contrary to what was intended by them: For the Arguments of the Deists which were quoted to be refuted, appeared to me much Stronger than the Refutations. In short I soon became a thorough Deist.

When a religion is good, I conceive it will support itself; and when it does not support itself, and God does not take care to support it so that its professors are obligated to call for help of the civil power, it's a sign, I apprehend, of its being a bad one.

CHAPTER 6
JAMES MADISON

Pops James

Another of my wishes is to depend as little as possible on the labor of slaves.[64]

BORN: March 16, 1751 in Port Conway, Virginia

DIED: June 28, 1836 in Orange, Virginia

AGE AT DEATH: 85

CAUSE OF DEATH: Heart failure, with complications from rheumatism and liver problems and/or gallbladder attacks. Madison was so sick in 1836 that he spent his final 6 months of life suffering in bed. He was not able to survive until the Fourth of July.[65]

POLITICAL PARTY: Democratic-Republican

FIRST LADY: Dorothy "Dolley" Payne Todd

CAREERS: Fourth president of the United States (1809–1817), member of the Continental Congress, member of the Constitutional Convention, author of the Bill of Rights, author of the United States Constitution

RELIGION: Episcopalian

NICKNAMES: Father of the Constitution, Jemmie, Little Jemmie, His Little Majesty

MEMORABLE QUOTES ABOUT HIM (AND DOLLEY): "James Madison, one of the pillars and ornaments of his country and of his age. His time on earth was short, yet he died full of years and of glory—less, far less than one hundred years have elapsed since the day of his birth—yet has he fulfilled, nobly fulfilled, his destinies as a man and a Christian. He has improved his own condition by improving that of his country and his kind."—John Quincy Adams[66]

[James Madison is] "a withered little applejohn." [Dolley Madison is a] "fine, portly, buxom dame."—Washington Irving, in a January, 1811 letter to Henry Brevort,

FOUNDING DOCUMENTS SIGNED: The United States Constitution

BOOKS TO READ FOR MORE INFORMATION:
- *James Madison* by Irving Brant
- *James Madison* by Richard Brookhiser
- *James Madison: A Life Reconsidered* by Lynne Cheney
- *James Madison and the Making of America* by Kevin Gutzm an
- *James Madison: A Biography* by Ralph Ketcham
- *Becoming Madison: The Extraordinary Origins of the Least Likely Founding Father* by Michael Signer

James Madison was diminutive, but he has an enormous legacy. He wrote the first drafts of the United States Constitution, created the Democratic-Republican Party, and was America's fourth president.

He helped author *The Federalist Papers*, started the War of 1812, and was a slaveholder.

He was a student of John Witherspoon at Princeton (see Chapter 31) and helped Thomas Jefferson start the University of Virginia.

He married Dolley Madison, and political writer George Will has said that Washington, D.C. should probably have been called "Madison, D.C."

Tall praise indeed for a not-so-tall man.

20 Things You Never Knew About James Madison

102. James Madison was 5'4" tall and didn't even weigh 100 pounds.
103. James Madison was either legitimately sickly, or a major league hypochondriac. [See *Revolutionary Medicine* for more.]
104. There was once an official $5,000 bill. James Madison was on it.
105. James Madison and George Washington were half first cousins, twice removed.
106. James Madison came up with the idea of renting Portugal's navy to fight for the U.S. in the War of 1812. He didn't want to spend any money building new battleships. That idea sunk like a stone.

107. We're not sure of James Madison's last words. They have been reported as "Nothing more than a change of mind, dear," and "I always talk better lying down."

108. James Madison went back to farming after he left the presidency in 1817 and experienced 9 total crop failures in 10 years. He become so desperate for money that he applied to the Bank of the United States for a $6,000 loan—and was turned down.

109. Thomas Jefferson held James Madison in extremely high regard. How high? He once told Benjamin Rush that Madison was "the greatest man in the world."[67]

Speaking words of wisdom . . .

110. "Conscience is the most sacred of all property."[68]

No wall for Madison . . .

111. "America was indebted to immigration for her settlement and prosperity. That part of America which had encouraged them most had advanced most rapidly in population, agriculture and the arts."[69]

Madison on power . . .

112. "All men having power ought to be distrusted to a certain degree."[70]

The madness of the crowd . . .

113. "The conduct of every popular assembly, acting on oath . . . shows that individuals join without remorse in acts against which their consciences would revolt, if proposed to them, separately, in their closets."[71]

The American conundrum . . .

114. "Every word of the Constitution decides a question between power and liberty."[72]

115. "Since the general civilization of mankind, I believe there are more instances of the abridgment of freedom of the people by gradual and silent encroachments of those in power, than by violent and sudden usurpations."[73]

116. "Wherever the real power in a government lies, there is the danger of oppression."[74]

117. "The essence of government is power; and power, lodged as it must be in human hands, will ever be liable to abuse."[75]

118. "The civil government functions with complete success by the total separation of the Church from the State."[76]

Women are smart . . . no doubt . . .

119. "The capacity of the female mind for studies of the highest order cannot be doubted, having been sufficiently illustrated by its works of genius, of erudition, and of science."[77]

But since we aren't angels . . .

120. "If men were angels, no government would be necessary. If angels were to govern men, neither external nor internal controls on government would be necessary. In farming a government which is to be administered by men over men, the great difficulty lies in this: you must first enable the government to control the governed; and the next place oblige it to control itself."[78]

121. "The power to declare war, including the power of judging the causes of war, is fully and exclusively vested in the legislature . . . the executive has no right, in any case, to decide the question, whether there is or is not cause for declaring war."[79]

An Interview with James Madison

Q: Good day, Mr. President, and may we express our sincere thanks to you for speaking with us today. It is a privilege to be with the man honored as the "Father of the United States Constitution."

A: The Constitution of the United States was created by the people of the United States composing the respective states, who alone had the right.

Q: How so?

A: Is it not the glory of the people of America, that, whilst they have paid a decent regard to the opinions of former times and other nations, they have not suffered a blind veneration for antiquity, for custom, or for names, to overrule the suggestions of their own good sense, the knowledge of their own situation, and the lessons of their own experience?

Q: Granted, but is there no risk in assigning this type of power to ordinary people?

A: A watchful eye must be kept on ourselves lest while we are building ideal monuments of Renown and Bliss here we neglect to have our names enrolled in the Annals of Heaven. The truth is that all men having power ought to be mistrusted.

Q: What are your thoughts on religion? Do you believe it is beneficial to mankind to believe in God and the other trappings of organized religions?

A: I have sometimes thought there could be no stronger testimony in favor of Religion or against temporal Enjoyments even the most rational and manly than for men who occupy the most honorable and gainful departments and are rising in reputation and wealth, publicly to declare their unsatisfactoriness by becoming fervent Advocates in the cause of Christ, & I wish you may give in your Evidence in this way. Such instances have seldom occurred, therefore they would be more striking and would be instead of a "Cloud of Witnesses."

Q: It seems clear that you do not support a national religion, nor a theocracy.

A: The Religion of every man must be left to the conviction and conscience of every man; and it is the right of every man to exercise it as these may dictate. Before any man can be considered as a member of Civil Society, he must be considered as a subject of the Governor of the Universe: And if a member of Civil Society, who enters into any subordinate Association, must always do it with a reservation of his duty to the general authority; much more must every man who becomes a member of any particular Civil Society, do it with a saving of his allegiance to the Universal Sovereign. We maintain therefore that in matters of Religion, no man's right is abridged by the institution of Civil Society, and that Religion is wholly exempt from its cognizance. The civil government functions with complete success by the total separation of the Church from the State.

Q: It has been said that one of America's "mortal sins" is the endorsement and practice of slavery. What are your thoughts on this abomination?

A: Slavery is, as you justly complain, a sad blot on our free country. Where slavery exists, the republican theory becomes still more fallacious. The United States, having been the first to abolish within the extent of their authority the transportation of the natives of Africa into slavery, by prohibiting the introduction of slaves and by punishing their citizens participating in the traffic, can not but be gratified at the progress made by concurrent efforts of other nations toward a general suppression of so great an evil.

CHAPTER 7
JOHN JAY

J. J.

Nothing is more certain than the indispensable necessity of government, and it is equally undeniable, that whenever and however it is instituted, the people must cede to it, some of their natural rights in order to vest it with requisite powers.[80]

BORN: December 12, 1745 in New York City, New York

DIED: May 17, 1829 in Bedford, New York

AGE AT DEATH: 83

CAUSE OF DEATH: Stroke. He had the stroke on May 14, 1829, and ended up severely paralyzed. He lived 3 days before dying on May 17, 1829.

POLITICAL PARTY: Federalist Party

WIFE: Sarah Livingston Jay

CAREERS: Governor of New York (2nd), first chief justice of the United States, United States secretary of foreign affairs, president of the Continental Congress (6th), delegate to the First and Second Constitutional Congresses

RELIGION: Episcopalian

NICKNAMES: None, but the CIA described him on their website as "the first national-level American counterintelligence chief."[81]

MEMORABLE QUOTE ABOUT HIM: "I have great confidence in the abilities, and purity of Mr. Jay's views, as well as in his experience."[82]

FOUNDING DOCUMENTS SIGNED: None.

BOOKS TO READ FOR MORE INFORMATION:
- *Founding Brothers: The Revolutionary Generation* by Joseph J. Ellis
- *The Quartet: Orchestrating the Second American Revolution, 1783-1789* by Joseph J. Ellis
- *John Jay* by Elbert Hubbard
- *John Jay: The Winning of the Peace, 1780-1784* by John Jay (Author), Richard B. Morris (Editor)
- *John Jay: The Forgotten Founder* by John M. Pafford
- *John Jay: Founding Father* by Walter Stahr

John Jay was a judge, a diplomat, a lawyer, a writer, and a co-author of the *Federalist Papers*. He signed the Treaty of Paris, and was appointed by George Washington himself as the first Supreme Court justice.

Quite a resume, eh?

John Jay was born in New York City into wealth. His father was a merchant and trader. His kids lived with Ben Franklin when Jay and his wife were in Paris, and two of his siblings lost their sight to smallpox.

John Jay was a slaveholder, but really didn't like the idea and was actually an abolitionist. In fact, he wrote an essay comparing colonial slaves to colonists themselves, with Great Britain being the slaveholder.

John Jay was one of the longest-lived Founders, dying at 83 of a stroke.

12 Things You Never Knew About John Jay

122. In 1783, John Jay was a member of the crew that brokered the Treaty of Paris, which effectively ended the Revolutionary War.
123. John Jay was the first United States Supreme Court justice.
124. John Jay abolished slavery in the state of New York when he was governor.
125. In 1794, John Jay was responsible for what became known as "Jay's Treaty," the "Treaty of Amity, Commerce, and Navigation, Between His Britannic Majesty and The United States of America." This treaty, which prevented yet another war with Great Britain, began with Article 1, "There shall be a firm inviolable and universal Peace, and a true and sincere Friendship between His Britannick Majesty, His Heirs and Successors, and the United States of America; and between their

respective Countries, Territories, Cities, Towns and People of every Degree, without Exception of Persons or Places." And for the most part, it worked.

126. John Jay was the author of 5 essays of *The Federalist Papers*, most of which were about foreign affairs.

127. John Jay was home-schooled, but later attended what is now Columbia University in New York City.

128. John Jay could be, to put it respectfully, "contentious" when he felt aggrieved. The story is told of an incident in his senior year at King's College. Some of Jay's classmates were screwing around, and one of them ended up destroying a dining room table. The president of the college, Dr. Myles Cooper, was beyond furious. He lined up the likely offenders and asked each of them if they had broken the table. They all said no. He then asked them if they knew who did break the table. Again, they all said no, except for John Jay. He knew who broke the table and declined to provide the president with the name of the guilty student. Cooper stormed out, but later, Jay was called before the scary big shots—the faculty members who would decide his fate. Prior to the interview, though, Jay reviewed all the college documents and rules and learned that there was no requirement for a student to rat out another student. He used this as his defense before the board . . . and they suspended him anyway. They did let him back in in time to graduate, though. (The college rules did include a caution against students behaving in a "contumacious" manner, but Jay dismissed that in his defense, possibly because he may not have known what it meant. Or if he did, he may not have been sure if breaking a dining room table qualified as contumacious behavior.)

Speaking words of wisdom . . .

The abolitionist . . .

129. "It is much to be wished that slavery may be abolished. The honour of the States, as well as justice and humanity, in my opinion, loudly call upon them to emancipate these unhappy people. To contend for our own liberty, and to deny that blessing to others, involves an inconsistency not to be excused."[83]

130. "But the safety of the people of America against dangers from foreign force depends not only on their forbearing to give just causes of war to

other nations, but also on their placing and continuing themselves in such a situation as not to invite hostility or insult; for it need not be observed that there are pretended as well as just causes of war."[84]

I'm busy establishing a new country, but I do miss you . . .

131. "[I have] a kind of confidence . . . that we shall yet enjoy many good days together, and I indulge myself in imaginary scenes of happiness which I expect in a few years to be realized. If it be a delusion, it is a pleasing one, and therefore I embrace it. Should it like a bubble vanish into air, resignation will blunt the edge of disappointment."[85]

132. "A treaty is only another name for a bargain; and that it would be impossible to find a nation who would make any bargain with us, which should be binding on them absolutely, but on us only so long and so far as we may think proper to be bound by it."[86]

Damn straight . . .

133. "Those who own the country ought to govern it." [87]

The Founders on Stage & Screen

There are 2 adages that speak the truth about writing, art, real life, and how the triad meet and intersect: Writers are always looking for ideas; truth is often stranger—and more compelling—than fiction.

The story of the American Revolution can be compared, in a sense, to the story of the *Titanic*. Imagine a writer walking into a Hollywood producer's office and saying the following:

> I've got the perfect idea! We tell the story of a company that decides to build the biggest ship in the world, stock it with millionaires for its maiden voyage . . . and then it hits an iceberg, breaks in half, and sinks 2 ½ miles down to the bottom of the ocean, killing fifteen hundred people!

Would such a pitch sell if the story of the *Titanic* had never happened?
The odds are "no."
It would seem too farfetched.
Yet, the *Titanic* script did happen precisely as described, and to this day, people are still ensorcelled with the story.

The story of the American Revolution has a similar "farfetched" feel to it: A ragtag band of colonists (they're always ragtag, right?) rebel against the most powerful empire in the world. And win.

And within a few decades, the 2 countries—the old one and the new one—are best of friends.

Irresistible, right?

For the past hundred years or so, this story has been told on stage, on TV, and in movies. Here's a look at some memorable efforts to recount the story of America.

TV

1954: *John Paul Jones* (TV movie)

1978: *The Bastard* (miniseries)

1979: *The Seekers* (miniseries)

1979: *The Rebels* (miniseries)

1994: *The American Revolution* (miniseries)

1997: *Thomas Jefferson* (documentary)

2006: *The Revolution* (miniseries)

2008: *John Adams* (miniseries)

2014: *The American Revolution* (miniseries)

2014: *Turn: Washington's Spies* (series)

2015: *Sons of Liberty* (miniseries)

STAGE

1964: *Ben Franklin in Paris*

1969: *1776*

1976: *The Ruckus at Machias*

2009: *A New World: A Life of Thomas Paine*

2015: *Jefferson's Garden*

2015: *Hamilton*

MOVIES

1909: *The Hessian Renegades*

1917: *Scouting for Washington*

1917: *The Spirit of '76*

1922: *Cardigan*

1924: *America*

1939: *Drums Along the Mohawk*

1939: *Sons of Liberty*

1940: *The Howards of Virginia*

1955: *The Scarlet Coat*

1957: *Johnny Tremain*

1957: *Williamsburg: the Story of a Patriot*

1959: *John Paul Jones*

1959: *The Devil's Disciple*

1961: *Lafayette*

1972: *1776*

1976: *Independence*

1985: *Revolution*

1987: *April Morning*

1987: *The Devil's Disciple*

2000: *The Crossing*

2000: *The Patriot*

2003: *Benedict Arnold: A Question of Honor*

2015: *Sons of Liberty*

CHAPTER 8
JAMES MONROE

Mr. Good Feelings

The best form of government is that which is most likely to prevent the greatest sum of evil.

BORN: April 28, 1758 in Monroe Hall, Virginia

DIED: July 4, 1831 in New York City, New York

AGE AT DEATH: 73

CAUSE OF DEATH: Heart failure with possible tuberculosis. In one of those incredible historical coincidences, Monroe was the 3rd of the first 5 U.S. presidents to die on the Fourth of July.

POLITICAL PARTY: Democratic-Republican

WIFE: Elizabeth "Eliza" Kortright

CAREERS: Farmer, lawyer, United States senator, 12th and 16th governor of Virginia, United States secretary of state, United States secretary of war

RELIGION: Episcopalian

NICKNAMES: The Era of Good Feelings President, The Last Cocked Hat

MEMORABLE QUOTE ABOUT HIM: "At the time of the Declaration of Independence, [Monroe was] in the process of completing his education at the college of William and Mary. He was then 17 years of age, and at the first formation of the American army entered it as a cadet. Had he been born 10 years before, it can scarcely be doubted that he would have been one of the members of the first Congress, and that his name would have gone down to posterity among those of 9 the signers of the Declaration of Independence."[88]

FOUNDING DOCUMENTS SIGNED: None

BOOKS TO READ FOR MORE INFORMATION:

- *James Monroe: The Quest for National Identity* by Harry Ammon
- *The Last Founding Father: James Monroe and a Nation's Call to Greatness* by Harlow Unger

T he Monroe Doctrine. Gaining Florida. The Missouri Compromise. The first senator president. The last Founding Father to be president. The last Founding Father to die. And even though the Monroe Doctrine was actually written by John Quincy Adams, it is James Monroe who is remembered for it. And considering it was the document that prohibited Europe from deciding to "acquire" any more American territory, it's quite a memorable legacy.

James Monroe was a slaveholder, too, but he equated it with "evil." When he died he was insolvent, but ultimately his wealth, or lack of it, had nothing to do with the profound impact he had on American history.

18 Things You Never Knew About James Monroe

134. James Monroe is the revolutionary holding the flag in the famous painting of Washington crossing the Delaware.
135. James Monroe is the Founder who bought Florida for the United States from Spain.
136. James Monroe voted against ratifying the U. S. Constitution. Why? He believed it made the Senate too powerful, and he didn't like the Electoral College.
137. "Mr. President" didn't work for James Monroe. His preferred form of address was "Colonel Monroe."
138. James Monroe is the only US president to have a foreign country's capital city named after him: Monrovia, Liberia.
139. James Monroe's presidential portrait was painted by Samuel Morse, the inventor of the Morse code. No, it was not a pointillist painting done in dots and dashes. (Sorry. That [bad] joke was just sitting there, and I couldn't resist.)

140. You're James Monroe's daughter. How would you feel if your father's favorite term of endearment for you was "My Little Monkey?"

141. James Monroe dropped out of the College of William and Mary to fight in the Revolutionary War under George Washington. He never went back to William and Mary, but he finished up his legal education under a pretty good teacher: Thomas Jefferson.

142. The first term of James Monroe's presidency was known as the "Era of Good Feelings." Why? We had just won the War of 1812, and there was only 1 political party in government. (*Sayonara* to the Federalists.) Monroe was re-elected almost unanimously, but that's not quite the amazing feat it sounds like when you're running unopposed.

143. When James Monroe visited Charleston, South Carolina by steamboat, the city roasted a whole ox in his honor.

Speaking words of wisdom . . .

Moving in . . . and up

144. "Our country may be likened to a new house. We lack many things, but we possess the most precious of all – liberty!"[89]

145. "If we look to the history of other nations, ancient or modern, we find no example of a growth so rapid, so gigantic, of a people so prosperous and happy." (From Monroe's first inaugural address)

Ignorance is dangerous . . .

146. "It is only when the people become ignorant and corrupt, when they degenerate into a populace, that they are incapable of exercising the sovereignty. Usurpation is then an easy attainment, and an usurper soon found. The people themselves become the willing instruments of their own debasement and ruin. Let us, then, look to the great cause, and endeavor to preserve it in full force. Let us by all wise and constitutional measures promote intelligence among the people as the best means of preserving our liberties."[90]

Monroe knew "you get what you pay for"

147. "To impose taxes when the public exigencies require them is an obligation of the most sacred character, especially with a free people." (From his First Annual Message, 1817)

Second Amendment fans love this quote . . .

148. "The right of self defense never ceases. It is among the most sacred, and alike necessary to nations and to individuals, and whether the attack be made by Spain herself or by those who abuse her power, its obligation is not the less strong."[91]

The U.S. population when he said this was less than 10 million . . .

149. "The great increase of our population throughout the Union will alone produce an important effect, and in no quarter will it be so sensibly felt as in those in contemplation."[92]

A classic definition of a self-fulfilling prophecy

150. "Preparation for war is a constant stimulus to suspicion and ill will."

Slavery = Evil

151. "What was the origin of our slave population? The evil commenced when we were in our Colonial state, but acts were passed by our Colonial Legislature, prohibiting the importation, of more slaves, into the Colony. These were rejected by the Crown. We declared our independence, and the prohibition of a further importation was among the first acts of state sovereignty. Virginia was the first state which instructed her delegates to declare the colonies independent. She braved all dangers. From Quebec to Boston, and from Boston to Savannah, Virginia shed the blood of her sons. No imputation then can be cast upon her in this matter. She did all that was in her power to do, to prevent the extension of slavery, and to mitigate its evils."[93]

WHAT DO THE 27 AMENDMENTS TO THE CONSTITUTION DO?

The Bill of Rights: Amendments 1–10

AMENDMENT #1: United States citizens have freedom of speech, religion, the press, to assemble, and the right to petition the government.

AMENDMENT #2: Grants United States citizens the right to bear arms.

AMENDMENT #3: The government cannot house soldiers in citizens' home during time of war.

AMENDMENT #4: There can be no unreasonable searches or seizures.

AMENDMENT #5: There can be no indictment without a grand jury; you can't be compelled to testify against yourself; you can't be tried twice for the same crime, i.e., no double jeopardy; you can't be taken into custody without due process; there can be no taking of private property without just compensation.

AMENDMENT #6: Grants United States citizens the right to a speedy trial and to be told of witnesses against them.

AMENDMENT #7: Grants United States citizens the right to a jury trial.

AMENDMENT #8: There can be no excessive bail; nor any cruel or unusual punishment.

AMENDMENT #9: Just because a right is not spelled out in the Constitution doesn't mean citizens don't have that right.

AMENDMENT #10: Any rights not delegated to the federal government belong to the people, i.e., the states.

AMENDMENT #11: Citizens cannot sue a state in federal court.

AMENDMENT #12: How to elect the president and vice president.

AMENDMENT #13: Abolished slavery.

AMENDMENT #14: The government cannot pass laws that deprive citizens of their civil rights, i.e., the right to due process, the right to vote, and so forth.

AMENDMENT #15: No rights can be denied to a person based on their race or color, or if they were previously a slave.

AMENDMENT #16: The government can collect taxes on income.

AMENDMENT #17: Senators are elected by the people.

AMENDMENT #18: Prohibition.

AMENDMENT #19: Women can vote.

AMENDMENT #20: Presidential and Congressional term lengths.

AMENDMENT #21: The repeal of Prohibition.

AMENDMENT #22: Presidents can serve only 2 terms.

AMENDMENT #23: People in Washington, D. C. can vote in federal elections.

AMENDMENT #24: Poll taxes cannot be charged in order to vote.

AMENDMENT #25: What happens if the President becomes disabled or dies while in office.

AMENDMENT #26: Eighteen-year olds can vote.

AMENDMENT #27: Pay raises for Congress cannot take effect until the next term.

CHAPTER 9
THOMAS PAINE

Makin' Sense

We have it in our power to begin the world again.[94]

BORN: February 9, 1737 in Thetford, Norfolk, England

DIED: June 8, 1809 in New York City, New York

AGE AT DEATH: 72

CAUSE OF DEATH: Natural causes, probably. An autopsy was not performed, and there is no record of what specifically killed him. Heart failure? Aneurysm? Undetected cancer? Truthfully, it's all speculation.

POLITICAL PARTY: None

WIVES: Elizabeth Ollive; Mary Lambert

CAREERS: Political activist, author of *The Rights of Man, The Age of Reason, The American Crisis*, and *Common Sense*, engineer, scientist, inventor

RELIGION: Deist

NICKNAMES: Father of the American Revolution,

MEMORABLE QUOTES ABOUT HIM: "Thomas Paine had passed the legendary limit of life. One by one most of his old friends and acquaintances had deserted him. Maligned on every side, execrated, shunned and abhorred – his virtues denounced as vices – his services forgotten – his character blackened, he preserved the poise and balance of his soul. He was a victim of the people, but his convictions remained unshaken. He was still a soldier in the army of freedom, and still tried to enlighten and civilize those who were impatiently waiting for his death."—Robert Ingersoll[95]

"I consider Paine our greatest political thinker. As we have not advanced, and perhaps never shall advance, beyond the Declaration and Constitution, so Paine has had no successors who extended his principles."—Thomas Edison[96]

"I never tire of reading Tom Paine."—Abraham Lincoln[97]

FOUNDING DOCUMENTS SIGNED: None

BOOKS TO READ FOR MORE INFORMATION:
- *Man of Reason: The Life of Thomas Paine* by Owen Aldridge
- *Thomas Paine* by A. J. Ayer
- *The Life of Thomas Paine* by Moncure Conway
- *Citizen Tom Paine* (historical novel) by Howard Fast
- *The Complete Writings of Thomas Paine*, Philip Foner, Ed.
- *Paine* by David Freeman Hawke
- *Thomas Paine: The Author of the Declaration of Independence* by Joseph L. Lewis
- *Thomas Paine: Enlightenment, Revolution, and the Birth of Modern Nations* by Craig Nelson
- *Tom Paine, The Greatest Exile* by David Powell

John Adams said about Paine that if Paine had not written *Common Sense* and *The American Crisis*, then "the sword of Washington would have been raised in vain."

Thomas Paine's writings were hugely successful, and he played a major role in making the American colonists ensorcelled with the notion of liberty. Paine is the guy who wrote what may be one of the greatest lines about troubled times ever: "These are the times that try men's souls."

Paine was unsuccessful in a variety of businesses and occupations as a young man, but he found his calling, and his voice, when he took a job editing the *Pennsylvania Magazine* (thanks to a push and a recommendation from Benjamin Franklin). He began writing incendiary essays anonymously or under a pseudonym, and it can be stated that he unequivocally changed the tenor of the times, and guided the emerging United States against the British.

27 Things You Never Knew About Thomas Paine

152. Paine was born in Thetford, England. His father was a Quaker and his mother was Anglican. Neither of these religions became part of Paine's personal ideology, and as an adult he was a Deist.

153. When he was living in England, Paine's wife and child both died in childbirth around 1760.

154. Paine was less than successful while living in England, and he moved to Philadelphia in 1774 Benjamin Franklin's urging. He immediately found employment as an editor of the *Pennsylvania Magazine*.

155. Paine was a passionate abolitionist. In March 1775, he published the 1600-word essay "African Slavery in America," which he addressed "To Americans." It is an important enough statement that we reprint it in this volume in its entirety. (See the essay in *The Reading Room*.)

156. Paine's *Common Sense* sold between 75,000 and 500,000 copies (depending on your source)[98] in 25 editions in 1776.

157. A lot of people did not like Thomas Paine. His antireligion philosophy in particular angered people. There were 6 mourners at his funeral.

158. Thomas Paine ended up in prison, sentenced to be guillotined for speaking out against the monarchy. This was considered treason and punishable by death. While in prison, he wrote the first part of *The Age of Reason*. He escaped death by a weird coincidence in which the white cross that was supposed to be painted on the cell doors of those who were to die the following day was placed in the wrong place and overlooked by the guards while collecting the doomed.

159. In 1792, Thomas Paine helped write the Constitution of France.

160. The domain of Paine's remains, remains a mystery. After his death in 1809, he was buried on his farm in New Rochelle, New York. Ten years later, one of Paine's arch-enemies (who later decided he adored Paine), William Cobbett, dug up Paine's remains and took them to England. He did not have permission from anyone, and his plans for a memorial to Paine fell through. Instead, pieces of Paine were sold off over the years. According to the *Associated Press*, "Parts of Paine might still be in England, possibly in the form of buttons made from his bones. There might be a rib in France. A man in Australia who claims to be a descendant says he has Paine's skull . . . . The only Paine parts that are still anywhere near the original burial site on his New Rochelle farm are his

mummified brain stem and a lock of hair that the historical association says it is keeping in a secret location."[99]

161. When Paine was 13, he and his father were stay makers. A stay is a thick rope used on sailing ships.

162. Paine's history of making stays with his father was twisted and used later by his enemies to impugn his and his father's reputations. His adversaries spread the word that the Paines were corset-makers. Apparently, that was considered a slur.

163. After Paine's stay-making business was over, he took a job as an excise officer, which was kind of like a tax enforcement officer. He was less than happy with the pay, though, so in 1772 he wrote a 21-page pamphlet called "The Case of the Officers of Excise." It was a rant for more pay. He was fired.

164. Paine's excise pamphlet complained about making 50 British pounds per year. How much would that be today? Maybe $5,000 or $6,000. I guess we can understand his gripe. He even figured out the take-home for illustration: "After tax, charity and sitting expenses are deducted there remains very little more than 46 pounds; and the expenses of horse-keeping in many places cannot be brought under 14 pounds a year, besides the purchase at first, and the hazard of life, which reduces it to 32 pounds per annum, or 1 shilling and 9 pence farthing per day."

165. "The Case of the Officers of Excise" was Paine's first published work. He was 35 years old.

166. After Edmund Burke wrote a raging essay against the French Revolution, Paine published *Rights of Man*, which railed against, well, all of European aristocracy. The book was banned in England and Paine was indicted for treason.

167. Thomas Paine has no direct descendants. He was an only child and never had children.

168. Over the centuries, many people have claimed descendancy from Thomas Paine, all of whose claims have been proven false. There has even been talk that Robert Treat Paine was either related to Thomas Paine, or was sometimes confused with Thomas Paine. There was no relation, and they were actually political enemies.

169. Thomas Paine makes an appearance of sorts in the smash Broadway musical *Hamilton*. In the song "The Schuyler Sisters," Angelica sings, "I've been reading Common Sense by Thomas Paine . . ."

Speaking words of wisdom . . .

Another Founder non-fan of religion . . .

170. "Of all the tyrannies that affect mankind, tyranny in religion is the worst."[100]

171. "Persecution is not an original feature in any religion; but it is always the strongly marked feature of all religions established by law. Take away the law-establishment, and every religion re-assumes its original benignity."[101]

Good advice . . .

172. "I love the man that can smile in trouble, that can gather strength from distress, and grow brave by reflection. 'Tis the business of little minds to shrink, but he whose heart is firm, and whose conscience approves his conduct, will pursue his principles unto death."[102]

173. "These are the times that try men's souls. The summer soldier and the sunshine patriot will, in this crisis, shrink from the service of his country, but he that stands it now, deserves the love and thanks of man and woman."[103]

Go, America!

174. "The Sun never shined on a cause of greater worth."[104]

175. "If we do not hang together, we shall surely hang separately."[105]

176. "Freedom had been hunted round the globe; reason was considered as rebellion; and the slavery of fear had made men afraid to think. But such is the irresistible nature of truth, that all it asks, and all it wants, is the liberty of appearing."[106]

Threaten Tom at your own risk . . .

177. "Not all the treasures of the world, so far as I believe, could have induced me to support an offensive war, for I think it murder; but if a thief breaks into my house, burns and destroys my property, and kills or threatens to kill me, or those that are in it, and to 'bind me in all cases whatsoever' to his absolute will, am I to suffer it?"[107]

> **Thomas Paine, Inventor**
>
> Thomas Paine, in addition to being a profoundly inspirational writer who contributed to the success of the American Revolution, was also an engineer, scientist, and inventor.
>
> He designed the River Bridge in Philadelphia and the Sunderland Bridge in Wearmouth, England, and he invented the smokeless candle.

Tom wasn't a fan of government either . . .

178. "Society in every state is a blessing, but government, even in its best state, is but a necessary evil; in its worst state an intolerable one; for when we suffer or are exposed to the same miseries by a government, which we might expect in a country without government, our calamity is heightened by reflecting that we furnish the means by which we suffer."[108]

An Interview with Thomas Paine

Q: **Good afternoon, Sir. May we begin by asking what you think of Great Britain?**

A: If ever a nation was was made foolish, and blind to its own interest and bent on its own destruction, it is Britain. There are such things as national sins, and though the punishment of individuals may be reserved to another world, national punishment can only be inflicted in this world. Britain, as a nation, is, in my inmost belief, the greatest and most ungrateful offender against God on the face of the whole earth. Blessed with all the commerce she could wish for, and furnished, by a vast extension of dominion, with the means of civilizing both the eastern and western world, she has made no other use of both than proudly to idolize her own "thunder," and rip up the bowels of whole countries for what she could get.

Q: **You reject King George's claim to the colonies, then?**

A: America, till now, could never be called a free country, because her legislation depended on the will of a man 3,000 miles distant, whose interest was in opposition to ours, and who, by a single "no," could forbid what law he pleased.

It is impossible that any country can flourish, as it otherwise might do, whose commerce is engrossed, cramped and fettered by the laws and mandates of another — yet these evils, and more than I can here enumerate, the continent has suffered by being under the government of England.

Q: **What do you think of British General William Howe, the commander who, at one point, supported the American colonies?**

A: To argue with a man who has renounced the use and authority of reason, and whose philosophy consists in holding humanity in contempt, is like administering medicine to the dead, or endeavoring to convert an atheist by scripture.

Q: **What do you think is the common perception among the British people regarding the colonies and the fight for independence?**

A: When information is withheld, ignorance becomes a reasonable excuse; and one would charitably hope that the people of England do not encourage cruelty from choice but from mistake. Their recluse situation, surrounded by the sea, preserves them from the calamities of war, and keeps them in the dark as to the conduct of their own armies. They see not, therefore they feel not. They tell the tale that is told them and believe it, and accustomed to no other news than their own, they receive it, stripped of its horrors and prepared for the palate of the nation, through the channel of the *London Gazette*. They are made to believe that their generals and armies differ from those of other nations, and have nothing of rudeness or barbarity in them. They suppose them what they wish them to be. They feel a disgrace in thinking otherwise, and naturally encourage the belief from a partiality to themselves.

Q: **You have become quite well known from your writings—*Common Sense, The American Crisis, The Rights of Man*, and so forth. Why did you begin writing with such prolificacy?**

A: It was the cause of America that made me an author. The force with which it struck my mind and the dangerous condition the country appeared to me in, by courting an impossible and an unnatural reconciliation with those who were determined to reduce her, instead of striking out into the only line that could cement and save her, A DECLARATION OF INDEPENDENCE, made it impossible for me, feeling as I did, to be silent: and if, in the course of more than seven years, I have rendered her any service, I have likewise added something to the reputation of literature, by freely and disinterestedly employing it in the great cause of mankind, and showing that there may be genius without prostitution.

Chapter 10
Patrick Henry

I Will Be Free!

Has Great Britain any enemy, in this quarter of the world, to call for all this accumulation of navies and armies? No, sir, she has none. They are meant for us; they can be meant for no other.[109]

Born: May 29, 1736 in Studley, Virginia

Died: June 6, 1799 in Brookneal, Virginia

Age at Death: 63

Cause of Death: Stomach cancer.

Political Parties: Federalist Party, Anti-Federalist, Anti-Administration

Wives: Dorothea Dandridge; Sarah Shelton

Careers: Governor of Virginia (1st and 6th), lawyer, tobacco farmer

Religion: Roman Catholic

Nicknames: Voice of the Revolution, Trumpet of the Revolution

Memorable Quote About Him: "His eloquence was peculiar, if indeed it should be called eloquence; for it was impressive and sublime, beyond what can be imagined. Although it was difficult when he had spoken to tell what he had said, yet, while he was speaking, it always seemed directly to the point."—Thomas Jefferson[110]

Founding Documents Signed: None

Books To Read For More Information:
- *Patrick Henry: A Biography* by Richard Beeman
- *Patrick Henry: First Among Patriots* by Thomas S. Kidd

- *Son of Thunder: Patrick Henry and the American Republic* by Henry Mayer
- *Patrick Henry: Patriot in the Making* by Robert D. Meade
- *Patrick Henry: Practical Revolutionary* by Robert D. Meade
- *Lion of Liberty: Patrick Henry and the Call To a New Nation* by Harlow Unger
- *Patrick Henry, Life, Correspondence, and Speeches* edited by William Wirt Henry

Born in Virginia to a Scottish immigrant father, Patrick Henry is a major American historical figure and voice for the revolution, thanks to one simple but incredibly powerful declaration: "Give me liberty or give me death!" (See an excerpt from Patrick Henry's "Give Me Liberty or Give Me Death!" Speech in "The Reading Room")

Patrick Henry died of stomach cancer before he could take his seat in the Virginia House of Delegates. In his will, he freed his slaves.

15 Things You Never Knew About Patrick Henry

179. Patrick Henry did not support the Constitution and did not sign it. He felt it infringed both states' and people's rights. He did support the Bill of Rights, though. Regarding the Constitution, he had this to say:

> My political curiosity, exclusive of my anxious solicitude for the public welfare, leads me to ask who authorised them to speak the language of, *We, the People,* instead of *We, the States?* States are the characteristics, and the soul of a confederation. If the States be not the agents of this compact, it must be one great consolidated National Government of the people of all the States.[111]

180. When Patrick Henry married Sarah Shelton in 1754, her father's wedding gift to the happy couple consisted of 6 slaves and a 600-acre plantation, Pine Slash Plantation.

181. Patrick Henry became a lawyer by persuading the governing panel that he would be a good one. He was self-taught, had no law experience, and had never been involved in a trial, but he convinced them that his intelligence alone was enough to assure his excellence as a practicing lawyer. They went for it.

182. Clergy and public officials in colonial Virginia were paid in tobacco. They received 16,000 pounds of tobacco worth 2 cents per pound, which mean they could sell it for $320. The price went to 6 cents per pound due to a drought, but Virginia passed a law that said the price of tobacco had to remain at 2 cents per pound. England overruled Virginia, but Patrick Henry successfully defended the state when a group of parsons sued. This victory established his legal career and set him up for a future political career.

183. Patrick Henry was fecund. He fathered 17 children with 2 wives.

184. Patrick Henry's wife Sarah developed what would today be diagnosed as a severe mental illness, believed to be puerperal (or postpartum) psychosis, a range of mental illness often following childbirth. Rather than lock her up in a filthy psychiatric "hospital," Patrick built her an apartment and cared for her until her death.

185. Sarah Henry was refused a Christian burial because it was believed her illness was caused by being possessed by the devil.

186. In 1955, the United States Postal Service issued a $1 "Patrick Henry" postage stamp. American artist Alonzo Chappel painted the portrait of Henry used on the stamp.

187. Patrick Henry has named for him, in addition to buildings, schools, ships, and places, a nuclear missile submarine, the *USS Patrick Henry*.

Speaking words of wisdom . . .

188. "Give me liberty or give me death!" (The fiery culmination to his speech delivered at the Second Virginia Convention, March 23, 1775)

189. "Perfect freedom is as necessary to the health and vigor of commerce as it is to the health and vigor of citizenship."

190. "Suspicion is a virtue as long as its object is the public good, and as long as it stays within proper bounds . . . Guard with jealous attention the public liberty. Suspect every one who approaches that jewel."[112]

Can't help but suspect that Pat was kind of religious . . .

191. "The Bible is worth all the other books which have ever been printed."

192. "A general toleration of Religion appears to me the best means of peopling our country. . . The free exercise of religion hath stocked the Northern part of the continent with inhabitants; and altho' Europe hath in great measure adopted a more moderate policy, yet the profession

of Protestantism is extremely inconvenient in many places there. A Calvinist, a Lutheran, or Quaker, who hath felt these inconveniences in Europe, sails not to Virginia, where they are felt perhaps in a (greater degree)."[113]

Slavery is bad, but . . .

193. "In this state there are 236,000 blacks, and there are many in several other states. But there are few or none in the Northern States; and yet, if the Northern States shall be of opinion that our slaves are numberless, they may call forth every national resource. May Congress not say, that every black man must fight? Did we not see a little of this last war? We were not so hard pushed as to make emancipation general; but acts of Assembly passed that every slave who would go to the army should be free. Another thing will contribute to bring this event about. Slavery is detested. We feel its fatal effects—we deplore it with all the pity of humanity. Let all these considerations, at some future period, press with full force on the minds of Congress. Let that urbanity, which I trust will distinguish America, and the necessity of national defence,—let all these things operate on their minds; they will search that paper, and see if they have power of manumission. And have they not, sir? Have they not power to provide for the general defence and welfare? May they not think that these call for the abolition of slavery? May they not pronounce all slaves free, and will they not be warranted by that power? This is no ambiguous implication or logical deduction. The paper speaks to the point: they have the power in clear, unequivocal terms, and will clearly and certainly exercise it. As much as I deplore slavery, I see that prudence forbids its abolition. I deny that the general government ought to set them free, because a decided majority of the states have not the ties of sympathy and fellow-feeling for those whose interest would be affected by their emancipation. The majority of Congress is to the north, and the slaves are to the south." [114]

An Interview with Patrick Henry

Q: What are your thoughts about our new Constitution?

A: The Constitution is not an instrument for the government to restrain the people, it is an instrument for the people to restrain the government—lest it come to dominate our lives and interests.

Q: So you don't put much trust in government, then, do you, sir?

A: The liberties of a people never were, nor ever will be, secure when the transactions of their rulers may be concealed from them. Show me that age and country where the rights and liberties of the people were placed on the sole chance of their rulers being good men, without a consequent loss of liberty?

Q: How can you be so certain that corruption will ensue?

A: I have but one lamp by which my feet are guided; and that is the lamp of experience. I know of no way of judging of the future but by the past.

Q: So, in your view, the Revolution was a necessary step to take?

A: Three millions of people, armed in the holy cause of liberty, and in such a country as that which we possess, are invincible by any force which our enemy can send against us. Beside, sir, we shall not fight our battles alone. There is a just God who presides over the destinies of Nations, and who will raise up friends to fight our battles for us.

Q: Many are afraid these days. Many feel insecure. What would you say to those who fear the future?

A: I know of no danger awaiting us. Public and private security are to be found here in the highest degree. Sir, it is the fortune of a free people not to be intimidated by imaginary dangers. Fear is the passion of slaves. Our political and natural hemisphere are now equally tranquil. Let us recollect the awful magnitude of the subject of our deliberation; let us consider the latent consequences of an erroneous decision, and let not our minds be led away by unfair misrepresentations and uncandid suggestions.

Q: Do you support the establishment of a Bill of Rights?

A: The necessity of a bill of rights appears to me to be greater in this government than ever it was in any government before. I have observed already, that the sense of the European nations, and particularly Great Britain, is against the construction of rights being retained which are not expressly relinquished. I repeat, that all nations have adopted this construction — that all rights not expressly and unequivocally reserved to the people are impliedly and incidentally relinquished to rulers, as necessarily inseparable from the delegated powers.

Q: You mention a "just God." I believe you are a Christian. What is it about Christianity that appeals to you?

A: I wish you to observe how real and beneficial the religion of Christ is to a man about to die. I have now disposed of all my property to my family. There is one thing more

I wish I could give them, and that is the Christian Religion. If they had that and I had not given them 1 shilling they would have been rich; and if they had not that and I had given them all the world, they would be poor. I am, however, much consoled by reflecting that the religion of Christ has, from its first appearance in the world, been attacked in vain by all the wits, philosophers, and wise ones, aided by every power of man, and its triumphs have been complete.

Q: You are a very forthright speaker. Does that come from your Virginian upbringing?

A: I am not a Virginian; I am an American. Should I keep back my opinions at such a time, through fear of giving offense, I should consider myself as guilty of treason toward my country, and of an act of disloyalty toward the majesty of heaven, which I revere above all earthly kings.

CHAPTER 11
SAMUEL ADAMS

The Brewmaster and Beyond

We cannot make events. Our business is wisely to improve them.[115]

BORN: September 27, 1722 in Boston, Massachusetts

DIED: October 2, 1803 in Cambridge, Massachusetts

AGE AT DEATH: 81

CAUSE OF DEATH: Complications from essential tremor, a debilitating, progressive disease that restricts movement.

POLITICAL PARTY: Democratic-Republican

WIVES: Elizabeth Wells; Elizabeth Checkley

CAREERS: Tax collector of Boston, 4th governor of Massachusetts, delegate to the Continental Congress

RELIGION: Congregationalist

NICKNAMES: Father of the American Revolution, Patriarch of Liberty, Firebrand of the Revolution

MEMORABLE QUOTE ABOUT HIM: "He organized the Revolution And Signed The Declaration of Independence—A Statesman Incorruptible and Fearless."—Written on the statue of Samuel Adams in front of Faneuil Hall in Boston, Massachusetts

FOUNDING DOCUMENTS SIGNED: Declaration of Independence, Articles of Confederation

BOOKS TO READ FOR MORE INFORMATION:
- *Samuel Adams: America's Revolutionary Politician* by John K. Alexander
- *The Sons of Liberty: The Lives and Legacies of John Adams, Samuel Adams, Paul Revere and John Hancock* by Charles River Editors

- *Samuel Adams* by James Kendall Hosmer
- *Samuel Adams: Father of the American Revolution* by Mark Puls
- *Desperate Sons: Samuel Adams, Patrick Henry, John Hancock, and the Secret Bands of Radicals Who Led the Colonies to War* by Les Stanford
- *Samuel Adams: A Life* by Ira Stoll
- *The Life and Public Services of Samuel Adams* by William Wells

Samuel Adams was a governor, a statesman, the cousin of a president, and a rabble-rouser. It takes a specific type of activist to meet the requirements for the eponym "rabble-rouser," and Samuel Adams qualified on all counts.

He had a hand in the Boston Tea Party, anti-Stamp Act resistance, anti-Boston occupation, and a slew of writings, letters, and speeches that made it perfectly clear that the British had to go and that America was a free country.

Yet to this day, Samuel Adams can be considered controversial. Regardless, he was a voice that changed things during a time when things needed changing.

16 Things You Never Knew About Samuel Adams

194. Samuel Adams and John Adams (2nd President of the United States) were second cousins.
195. Samuel Adams chaired the meeting that essentially pushed the "Start" button for the Boston Tea Party. He didn't come right out and say, "Go revolt," but instead gave a secret signal which consisted of him saying, "This meeting can do nothing more to save the country." That somewhat vague "message" did the trick, however, and the tossing overboard of sundry teas began shortly thereafter.
196. Samuel Adams was an ineffective businessman. After he was fired from a job in a counting house because his boss believed that he was more interested in the revolution against Great Britain, his father loaned him a thousand pounds to start his own business. He immediately re-loaned half of it to a friend (which he never got back, of course), and then spent the rest on mostly non-business pursuits.
197. Samuel Adams had a reputation of being . . . well, a slob. His clothes were commonly rumpled and dirty; he never changed his wig; his presentation was shabby and disheveled.
198. Samuel Adams' hatred for the King and the British government was personal: Out of the blue, England issued a decree that Adams' father's investments in Boston were illegal. The family was financially ruined.

199. Samuel Adams took a job as tax collector for Boston but was less than diligent about his duties. If you were his friend and you owed back taxes, he'd overlook the debt. If he collected money, he would carelessly keep it intermingled with his own personal money. (We cannot help but muse as to how many personal debts were "inadvertently" paid with Boston tax monies.) He also didn't keep careful records. This was known, both in Boston and Britain, and before long, he was audited and it was discovered he was 7,000 pounds short. John Hancock made good on the money on Adams's behalf.

200. Due to Adams's propagandizing against Britain, the king repealed the hated Stamp Act, but replaced it with even worse taxes and tariffs. Samuel Adams was furious and was responsible for organizing Boston's street gangs into a group called the Sons of Liberty. They used violence—tarring and fathering and arson, in particular—to make their point.

Speaking words of wisdom . . .

201. "Mankind are governed more by their feelings than by reason."[116]

202. "The truth is, all might be free if they valued freedom, and defended it as they ought."[117]

203. "We cannot make Events. Our Business is wisely to improve them. There has been much to do to confirm doubting Friends & fortify the Timid. It requires time to bring honest Men to think & determine alike even in important Matters. Mankind are governed more by their feelings than by reason."[118]

Vain & aspiring men . . .

204. "If ever the Time should come, when vain & aspiring Men shall possess the highest Seats in Government, our Country will stand in Need of its experienced Patriots to prevent its Ruin."[119]

The love of money . . .

205. "If ye love wealth better than liberty, the tranquility of servitude than the animating contest of freedom, go from us in peace. We ask not your counsels or arms. Crouch down and lick the hands which feed you. May your chains sit lightly upon you, and may posterity forget that ye were our countrymen."[120]

206. "Let each citizen remember at the moment he is offering his vote that he is not making a present or a compliment to please an individual—or

at least that he ought not so to do; but that he is executing one of the most solemn trusts in human society for which he is accountable to God and his country."[121]

Life, liberty, property . . . and guns

207. "Among the natural rights of the colonists are these: First a right to life, secondly to liberty, and thirdly to property; together with the right to defend them in the best manner they can."[122]
208. "In regard to religion, mutual toleration in the different professions thereof is what all good and candid minds in all ages have ever practiced, and both by precept and example inculcated on mankind."[123]

No taxation without . . . you know the rest

209. "For if our Trade may be taxed, why not our Lands? Why not the Produce of our Lands & everything we possess or make use of? This we apprehend annihilates our Charter Right to govern & tax ourselves. It strikes at our British privileges, which as we have never forfeited them, we hold in common with our Fellow Subjects who are Natives of Britain. If Taxes are laid upon us in any shape without our having a legal Representation where they are laid, are we not reduced from the Character of free Subjects to the miserable State of tributary Slaves?"[124]

CHAPTER 12
JOHN HANCOCK

Mr. Big Sig

Some boast of being friends to government; I am a friend to righteous government, to a government founded upon the principles of reason and justice; but I glory in publicly avowing my eternal enmity to tyranny.[125]

BORN: January 23, 1737 in Braintree, Massachusetts

DIED: October 8, 1793 in Boston, Massachusetts

AGE AT DEATH: 56

CAUSE OF DEATH: Natural causes. A definitive cause has never been discerned. Hancock suffered from gout and what has been described as "declining health" in the years prior to his death.

POLITICAL PARTY: None

WIFE: Dorothy Quincy

CAREERS: President of the Second Continental Congress, 1st and 3rd governor of Massachusetts

RELIGION: Congregationalist

NICKNAME: King Hancock

MEMORABLE QUOTE ABOUT HIM: "His reverence for religion was never lost. He was interested in every thing that related to the house of God. He exceeded his worthy ancestors in his liberality to this society and proved his real attachment to our peace and happiness. It might have been said of him as of the centurion by the Jews, 'He loved our nation and hath built us a synagogue.'"[126]

FOUNDING DOCUMENTS SIGNED: Articles of Confederation, Declaration of Independence

BOOKS TO READ FOR MORE INFORMATION:
- *John Hancock: Patriot in Purple* by Herbert Allan
- *John Hancock's Life and Speeches: A Personalized Vision of the American Revolution, 1763–1793* edited by Paul D. Brandes
- *John Hancock, His Book* [letters] edited by Abram E. Brown
- *The Baron of Beacon Hill: A Biography of John Hancock* by William M. Fowler, Jr.
- *John Hancock: Merchant King and American Patriot* by Harlow Unger
- *John Hancock, The Picturesque Patriot* by Lorenzo Sears

I f John Hancock's only legacy was that he was the first to sign the United States Constitution, we'd still be talking about him today.

But he was more than that and, it can be said, he should share the title of "rabble-rouser" with Samuel Adams.

He was a governor of Massachusetts (twice), was very wealthy, and was a smuggler. He used his wealth to curry favor and attention to the Revolutionary cause and died at the very young age of 56.

14 Things You Never Knew About John Hancock

210. When asked why his signature on the Declaration of Independence was so large, John Hancock joked that it was so King George would be able to read it without his glasses. (That may be an apocryphal story.) Historians today feel, however, that the oversized signature was a deliberate "statement" on his part, so to speak, of the incredibly high regard in which he held himself. (He had a bit of an ego, old JH did.)

211. John Hancock's signature on the Declaration of Independence was so memorable, the phrase "John Hancock" is now a synonym for "signature."

212. John Hancock suffered from a persistent and painful case of gout.

213. When John Hancock died, he was worth $350,000 in 1793 dollars. This is around $9 million dollars today. He was likely the richest Founding Father.

214. John Hancock's attorney was John Adams.

215. John Hancock enrolled in Harvard when he was thirteen years old.

216. During a 1760-1761 business trip to England, John Hancock witnessed the coronation of King George III on September 22, 1761. Hancock would later refuse allegiance to the King and participate in the war to wrest away his authority over the colonies. (Benjamin Franklin was also at the coronation ceremony, but Hancock didn't know him yet.)

Speaking words of wisdom . . .

We are the champions . . .

217. "I have the most animating confidence that the present noble struggle for liberty will terminate gloriously for America." [127]

218. "I mean not to boast; I would not excite envy, but manly emulation. We have all one common cause; let it, therefore, be our only contest, who shall most contribute to the security of the liberties of America. And may the same kind Providence which has watched over this country from her infant state still enable us to defeat our enemies!" [128]

Knowledge is power . . .

219. "The important consequences to the American States from this Declaration of Independence, considered as the ground and foundation of a future government, naturally suggest the propriety of proclaiming it in such a manner as that the people may be universally informed of it."[129]

JH was pro-Second Amendment . . .

220. "A well-disciplined militia is a safe, an honorable guard to a community like this, whose inhabitants are by nature brave, and are laudably tenacious of that freedom in which they were born. From a well-regulated militia we have nothing to fear; their interest is the same with that of the State. When a country is invaded, the militia are ready to appear in its defense; they march into the field with that fortitude which a consciousness of the justice of their cause inspires; they do not jeopard their lives for a master who considers them only as the instruments of his ambition, and whom they regard only as the daily dispenser of the scanty pittance of bread and water. No; they fight for their houses, their lands, for their wives, their children; for all who claim the tenderest names, and are held dearest in their hearts; they fight *pro aris et focis*, for their liberty, and for themselves, and for their God." [130]

Monied does not mean moral . . .

221. "People who pay greater respect to a wealthy villain than to an honest, upright man in poverty, almost deserve to be enslaved; they plainly show that wealth, however it may be acquired, is, in their esteem, to be preferred to virtue." [131]

Ned Ryerson? Bing!

222. "The greatest ability in business is to get along with others and to influence their actions. A chip on the shoulder is too heavy a piece of baggage to carry through life."

Yes, it sure does . . .

223. "I find money some way or other goes very fast. But I think I can reflect it has been spent with satisfaction and to my own honour."

How To Display The United States Constitution

Want to see the actual United States Constitution?

No problem.

Since 1952, the original United States Constitution has been on display at the National Archives Building in Washington, D.C.

It is well protected:

- The case in which the four pages of the Constitution are displayed is covered with protective glass framed with titanium. In this case, "protective" means protects against any dire attempts to break it: bullets, rocks, acid, etc.
- Argon gas fills the cases holding the Constitution. Oxygen would contribute to the degradation of the paper on which the Constitution is written. Argon prevents this.
- The interior temperature of the display case is 67 degrees Fahrenheit. Not 66, not 68, 24 hours a day, all year round.
- The interior relative humidity of the display case is 40 percent.

Part II

AN INVALUABLE: 20 FOUNDERS

William Blount ♦ Charles Carroll ♦ John Dickinson ♦ Elbridge Gerry ♦ Frances Hopkinson ♦ Rufus King ♦ Richard Henry Lee ♦ Robert R. Livingston ♦ John Marshall ♦ George Mason ♦ Gouverneur Morris ♦ Robert Morris ♦ William Paterson ♦ Charles Cotesworth Pinckney ♦ Charles Pinckney ♦ Benjamin Rush ♦ Roger Sherman ♦ James Wilson ♦ John Witherspoon ♦ George Wythe

CHAPTER 13
WILLIAM BLOUNT

Show Me Da Money

[I signed the Constitution to make it] the unanimous act of the States in Convention.[132]

BORN: March 26, 1749 in Windsor, North Carolina

DIED: March 21, 1800 in Knoxville, Tennessee

AGE AT DEATH: 50

CAUSE OF DEATH: Unspecified. In March of 1800, some type of "epidemic" assaulted Knoxville, Tennessee, sickening many people, including Blount's family. He, too, got sick and died ten days later. What could it have been? Flu? Smallpox? Some virus. We just don't know.

POLITICAL PARTY: Democratic-Republican

WIFE: Mary Grainger

CAREERS: United States senator from Tennessee, governor of the Southwest Territory, Continental Congressman from North Carolina

RELIGION: Presbyterian

NICKNAMES: None known

MEMORABLE QUOTE ABOUT HIM: "After a careful study of his life and character, I do not hesitate to say that in breadth of intellect, deep thought, untiring activity, intrepid perseverance, and broad patriotism lie had few equals and no superior among his colleagues."[133.]

FOUNDING DOCUMENTS SIGNED: The United States Constitution

BOOKS TO READ FOR MORE INFORMATION:
- *The Blount Journal 1790-1796* by William Blount
- *Letters of Governor William Blount,* edited by Philip M. Hamer
- *William Blount* by William Henry Masterson
- *Some Account of the Life and Services of William Blount* by General Marcus Wright

10 Things You Never Knew About William Blount

224. In 1797, Blount, then a U.S. senator, came up with a plan to conquer Florida and Louisiana (then controlled by Spain) for the British. He would use Indians, members of the British navy, and mercenaries. He wrote out his plan in a letter which ended up in the hands of President John Adams who, rather quickly, saw to it that the Senate "fired" him. This was known as "Blount's Conspiracy." It ruined his reputation.

225. While working as commissary to General Horatio Gates, Blount once lost $300,000 that was supposed to be used to pay soldiers. Apparently, he got flustered during the Battle of Camden and couldn't keep track of the cash.

226. Even though his name was tarnished by his actions in Blount's Conspiracy, William Blount is still held in very high regard in the South. He has towns, schools, and streets named for him in Tennessee and North Carolina, and his home, Blount's Mansion, is a National Historical Landmark and listed on the National Register of Historical Places.

227. In 1791, Blount and his family lived in a log cabin in 1791 after buying land in Tennessee in a land lottery.

228. When Blount built what became known as Blount's Mansion, people in the era were in awe at the sumptuous luxuriousness of the house, which ended up being Blount's center of business and living. One particular group that was absolutely astonished by the house were members of the local Native American tribes. Why? They had never seen a 2-story dwelling before.

229. When Blount entertained Native American tribe leaders at his mansion, he always treated them with the respect and deference he gave to other national leaders.

230. In January 1796, William Blount was the one who initiated and called to order the first Constitutional Convention.

Speaking Words of Wisdom . . .

The frontier beckons . . .

231. "The salary is handsome and my western lands had become so great an object to me that it had become absolutely necessary that I should go to the western country. . ."[134]

Trying to make the Indians happy . . .

232. "You may assure the Indians in the strongest Terms of good Treatment and I assure you it is their true Interest to come in and treat. I really wish they would so conduct themselves as that it may be in the Power of the United States to make them a much happier People than they are or can be if they do not treat."[135]

Trying to make the people happy . . .

233. "My object in administering the government has been to please the people as far as I could consistent with the duties I owed the federal government, having always in view their happiness. The pleasure of pleasing to me is a great one, but unmerited censure gives no pain except that of reflecting that it is drawn on me by the address of people who have not maturely thought on the subject, or have objects in view different from that of the public good."[136]

---

26 ITEMS ON A VALLEY FORGE GROCERY LIST

The Continental Army, led by George Washington, spent the winter of 1777–1778 at Valley Forge, Pennsylvania. They were cold, tired and, above all, hungry. They were so hungry, in fact, that George Washington himself wrote a letter to Henry Laurens, the president of Congress, warning him that if he did not get the supplies and foodstuffs he needed for his soldiers, "this Army must dissolve." He sent a shopping list to the Commissary department. These are the things the troops needed, and needed *now*. A great many of the items were unavailable, but Washington gave it his best shot. Note that of the 26 items on the list, three of them are alcoholic beverages.

1. Bacon
2. Beef
3. Bread
4. Butter
5. Cabbages
6. Cider
7. Fish
8. Flour
9. Hams
10. Lard
11. Molasses
12. Mutton
13. Peas
14. Pork
15. Potatoes
16. Rice
17. Rum
18. Salt
19. Slat Beef
20. Spirits
21. Tongues
22. Turnips
23. Veal
24. Vinegar
25. Wheat
26. Whiskey

CHAPTER 14
CHARLES CARROLL
OF CARROLLTON

The Catholic

Necessity, says ye proverb, is ye mother of invention.[137]

BORN: September 19, 1737 in Annapolis, Maryland

DIED: November 14, 1832 in Baltimore, Maryland

AGE AT DEATH: 95

CAUSE OF DEATH: Unknown, but contemporary writings indicate he suffered from "poor health."

POLITICAL PARTY: Federalist Party

WIFE: Mary Darnell

CAREERS: United States senator from Maryland (1789-1792)

RELIGION: Roman Catholic

MEMORABLE QUOTES ABOUT HIM: John Adams said (I'm paraphrasing): of all the great men of this time period, only Washington would be more remembered than Charles Carroll.[138]

"When I first saw Mr. Carroll, he was in his 86th year. He lived ten years longer. Below the middle size, weak and emaciated, his voice thin and feeble, writing with a trembling hand, but always signing his name 'Charles Carroll of Carrollton,' you saw in him, as he approached to greet you, a very feeble and aged man. His hair was scant and white and silky, and his eyes especially were suggestive of great age. His complexion, however, was healthy, and tremulous as were his movements, they were quick. His hearing was but little affected by his years and he listened with apparent eagerness to all that was said in his presence. His dress was the knee breeches of the old school, when I first recollect him, his waistcoat as long as we see in oldtime pictures, and I never saw him except in a loose roquelaure, something between a dressing gown and a frock coat. His manners were charming, his countenance pleasant and sprightly, and as one looked at Mr. Carroll, one saw a shadow from past days, when manner was cultivated as essential to a gentleman."[139]

FOUNDING DOCUMENTS SIGNED: Declaration of Independence

BOOKS TO READ FOR MORE INFORMATION:
- *American Cicero: The Life of Charles Carroll* by Bradley J. Birzer
- *Unpublished Letters of Charles Carroll of Carrollton and of his Father, Charles Carroll of Doughoregan* by Charles Carroll
- *Life of Charles Carroll of Carrollton* by Lewis A. Leonard
- *Charles Carroll of Carrollton: Faithful Revolutionary* by Scott McDermott
- *The Life of Charles Carroll of Carrollton* by Kate Mason Rowland
- *Charles Carroll of Carrollton* by Ellen Hart Smith

16 Things You Never Knew About Charles Carroll of Carrollton

234. Charles Carroll of Carrollton (which is how he officially signed his name) was a bastard. His father was Charles Carroll of Annapolis; his mother was Elizabeth Brooke. His father refused to marry his mother for fear that if he died first, Elizabeth Brooke would end up with the family's estate and money and give it to the guy she (he was certain) would later marry. Ah, true love.

235. In 1776, Charles Carroll traveled to Canada to try to convince the Canadians to join the cause and fight on the side of the Colonies in the Revolutionary War. He was (utterly) unsuccessful.

236. In the summer of 1774, a British ship loaded with tea arrived at Annapolis, Maryland. In June of that year, however, the Maryland legislature had passed a law banning the importation of British tea. As soon as the people of Annapolis learned that there was a ship in port carrying the now illegal brew, huge crowds gathered at the shore, vociferously

proclaiming all manner of mayhem upon the ship, her captain, and her crew. It became clear that the life of the Captain was at risk. Concerned friends of the seafarers appealed to the highly-regarded and highly-respected Charles Carroll for help. Carroll was willing, but he knew that the crowd was so passionate and angry that words probably would not solve the problem. So he came up with what can perhaps be called an ingenious—if harsh—solution. He convinced the Captain to set fire to his own ship. The Captain set its sails and immolated his own vessel. This satisfied the crowd, and the Captain was not harmed.

237. Charles Carroll was the last signer of the Declaration of Independence to die.

238. Carroll Hall at the University of Notre Dame is named after Charles Carroll.

239. Charles Carroll was one of the founders of Georgetown University.

240. Charles Carroll did not cotton to the idea of Thomas Jefferson as president of the United States. The following is an excerpt from a letter from Carroll to Alexander Hamilton:

> Dear Sir:
>
> It is asserted with confidence by the Anti-federal party here, that all your electors will vote for Mr. Jefferson as President. If such an event should really happen, it is probable he will be chosen. Of such a choice, the consequences to this country may be dreadful. Mr. Jefferson is too theoretical and fanciful a statesman to direct with steadiness and prudence the affairs of this extensive and growing confederacy. He might safely try his experiments, without much inconvenience in the little republic of St. Marino, but his fantastic tricks would dissolve this Union.[140]

241. When Charles Carroll signed the Declaration of Independence, he was the wealthiest of all the signers and came from the wealthiest family in America.

242. During the Revolutionary War, Charles Carroll paid for Irish men to come to America and fight on the side of the Colonies.

243. Much of what is Washington, D.C. today is land that was donated by Charles Carroll.

244. Ever play Monopoly? Thank Charles Carroll for his founding of the B&O Railroad, which appears on the Monopoly game board.

Speaking Words of Wisdom . . .

245. "Designing and selfish men invented religious tests to exclude from posts of profit and trust their weaker or more conscientious fellow subjects, thus to secure to themselves all the emoluments of Government."[141]

Give until it hurts . . .

246. "All believing in the religion of Christ may practice the leading principle of charity, the basis of every virtue."[142]

247. "Whatever threats are thrown out or force employed to make ye Americans as compliant as ye Parliament, they will never depart from the essential right of internal taxation without which our property would be at ye mercy of every rapacious minister."[143]

CC loved the ladies . . .

248. "What happiness on earth without the ladies? They polish, and soften ye manners; in their company the Englishman, such is the force of beauty and of with, slights his tobacco-pipe and coffee house politics; reduced to defend his own heart, he forgets his speculative battles; for my own part I can't conceive how my heart remains still unsubdued."[144]

249. "In these times of necessity and oppression it is a duty every man of fortune owes his country to set an example of frugality and industry to ye common people: 'Necessity,' says ye proverb, 'is ye mother of invention,' and my add of industry." [145]

THE MUSICAL FOUNDERS

Thomas Jefferson said music was "the favorite passion of my soul." Benjamin Franklin was a multi-instrumentalist. Francis Hopkinson invented a musical instrument, the Bellarmonic, a modification of the glass harmonica. This feature looks at 6 Founders who played musical instruments. (I wonder if they ever got together and jammed.)

- George Washington: flute
- Thomas Jefferson: violin, cello, clavichord
- Patrick Henry: violin, flute, fiddle
- Benjamin Franklin: violin, cello, viola, guitar, harp, harpsichord, bells, glass armonica
- Francis Hopkinson: harpsichord, Bellarmonic
- George Wythe: violin

CHAPTER 15
JOHN DICKINSON

The Penman

In Freedom we're born and in Freedom we'll live.[146]

Dickinson was not a mere lawyer in the sense that he adopted the calling in order to make a livelihood. He was a man of statesmanlike mind, and, no doubt, ambitious of distinction in public life.[147]

BORN: November 13 or 15, 1732 in Talbot County, Maryland

DIED: February 14, 1808 in Wilmington, Delaware

AGE AT DEATH: 75

CAUSE OF DEATH: Unknown

POLITICAL PARTY: Democratic-Republican

WIFE: Mary "Polly" Norris

CAREERS: 5th president of Pennsylvania, president of Delaware, Continental Congressman, journalist

RELIGION: Quaker

NICKNAMES: Penman of the Revolution, Fabius, Farmer

MEMORABLE QUOTE ABOUT HIM: "A more estimable man or truer patriot could not have left us. Among the first of the advocates for the rights of his country when assailed by Great Britain, he continued to the last the orthodox advocate of the true principles of our new government, and his name will be consecrated in history as one of the great worthies of the Revolution."—Thomas Jefferson[148]

> FOUNDING DOCUMENTS SIGNED: The Articles of Confederation, the United States Constitution (by George Read on Dickinson's behalf)
>
> BOOKS TO READ FOR MORE INFORMATION:
> - *John Dickinson: Conservative Revolutionary* by Milton E. Flower
> - *Democracy in Delaware* by Carol E. Hoffecker
> - *History of Delaware Through Its Governors* by Roger A. Martin
> - *Philadelawareans* by John A. Munroe
> - *The Life and Times of John Dickinson* by Charles J. Stillé

10 Things You Never Knew About John Dickinson

250. John Dickinson concluded each of his brilliant series of letters called *Letters from a Farmer in Pennsylvania* with a Latin quote and its English translation. Each quote spoke to the theme of the letter.

Letter 1

Concordia res parvae crescunt.

Small things grow great by concord.

Letter 2

Vox et praeterea nihil.

A sound and nothing else.

Letter 3

Nil desperandum.

Nothing is to be despaired of.

Letter 4

Habemus quidem senatus consultum, tanquam gladium in vagina repositum.

We have a statute, laid up for future use, like a sword in the scabbard.

Letter 5

Mens ubi materna est?

Where is maternal affection?

Letter 6

Quocirca vivite fortes Fortiaque adversis opponite pectora rebus.

Wherefore keep up your spirits, and gallantly oppose
this adverse course of affairs.

Letter 7

Miserabile vulgus.

A miserable tribe.

Letter 8

Qui sentit commodum, sentire debet et onus.

They who feel the benefit, ought to feel the burden.

Letter 9

Venienti occurrite morbo.

Oppose a disease at its beginning.

Letter 10

Et majores vestros & posteros cogitate.

Remember your ancestors and your posterity.

Letter 11

Infelix vates.

A direful foreteller of future calamities.

Letter 12

*Certe ego libertatem, quae mihi a parente meo tradita est, experiar: "Verum
id frustra an ob rem faciam, in vestra manu situm est, quirites."*

For my part, I am resolved to contend for the liberty
delivered down to me by my ancestors, but whether I shall
do it effectually or not, depends on you, my countrymen.
"How littlesoever one is able to write, yet when the liberties
of one's country are threatened, it is still more difficult to be silent."

251. John Dickinson was the lyricist of "The Liberty Song," one of the first "pro-America" patriotic songs of the Revolutionary era.

252. John Dickinson was not a fan of horse-drawn carriages. In an October 1777 letter to his wife after the British had occupied Philadelphia, he requested she come to him as soon as possible, and was very clear about her mode of travel: "I dread your coming in a 2-wheeled carriage. If any of your friends supply you with horses they shall be well taken care of." It's interesting that this last sentence leaves open whether it's the friends or the horses that will be "well taken care of." [149]

253. From 1781 through 1785, John Dickinson was simultaneously the governor of both Delaware and Pennsylvania. (Although back then, governors of states were known as "president," as in "president of Delaware" and "president of Pennsylvania.")

254. John Dickinson wrote the second draft of the Olive Branch Petition, a final entreaty to King George III from members of the Second Continental Congress. This petition demanded that the King, essentially, back off and leave the colonies and the colonists alone and address their grievances, most of which were financial and tax-related. He was unctuous and conciliatory in the piece, and referred to the "still faithful Colonists" and your "faithful subjects of the Colonies." The Petition did not do a lot of good, and we cannot help but muse on what might have been the response had they sent the original draft, written by Thomas Jefferson (along with Benjamin Franklin and John Jay, among others), which Dickinson rewrote because he felt Jefferson's language was too harsh. King George issued a response (even though he never even read the Petition), and it was nasty: anyone talking about severing ties with the Crown was in rebellion and in his response, called, fittingly, the Declaration of Rebellion, he said, "We do accordingly strictly charge and command all our Officers, as well civil as military, and all others our obedient and loyal subjects, to use their utmost endeavors to withstand and suppress such rebellion, and to disclose and make known all treasons and traitorous conspiracies which they shall know to be against us, our crown and dignity; and for that purpose, that they transmit to one of our principal Secretaries of State, or other proper officer, due and full information of all persons who shall be found carrying on correspondence with, or in any manner or degree aiding or abetting the persons now in open arms and rebellion against our Government, within any of our Colonies and Plantations in North America, in order

to bring to condign punishment the authors, perpetrators, and abettors of such traitorous designs." The Second Continental Congress responded to the Declaration with a missive stating that any assaults, punishments, attacks, or mistreatments "shall be retaliated in the same kind." The Olive Branch Petition and its response and counter-response were one of the leading causes of the American Revolution.

Speaking Words of Wisdom . . .

255. "An act of parliament, commanding us to do a certain thing, if it has any validity, is a tax upon us for the expense that accrues in complying with it; and for this reason, I believe, every colony on the continent, that chose to give a mark of their respect for Great Britain, in complying with the act relating to the troops, cautiously avoided the mention of that act, lest their conduct should be attributed to its supposed obligation."[150]

256. "If the parliament may lawfully deprive New York of any of her rights, it may deprive any, or all the other colonies of their rights; and nothing can possibly so much encourage such attempts, as a mutual inattention to the interests of each other."[151]

Because I'm Happy . . .

257. "We cannot be happy without being free, we cannot be free without being secure in our property, we cannot be secure in our property, if, without our consent, others may, as by right, take it away. Taxes imposed on us by parliament, do thus take it away—duties laid for the sole purpose of raising money, are taxes—attempts to lay such duties should be instantly and firmly opposed."[152]

258. "Experience must be our only guide. Reason may mislead us. It was not Reason that discovered the singular and admirable mechanism of the British Constitution."[153]

259. "It was not reason that discovered the singular and admirable mechanism of the English Constitution . . . [or the] mode of trial by jury. Accidents probably produced these discoveries, and experience has given a sanction to them. Then this was our guide."[154]

Chapter 16
Elbridge Gerry

Gerrymander This!

[I]t must be admitted, that a free people are the proper guardians of their rights and liberties—that the greatest men may err and that their errors are sometimes of the greatest magnitude.[155]

Born: July 17, 1744 in Marblehead, Massachusetts

Died: November 23, 1814 in Washington, D.C.

Age at Death: 70

Cause of Death: Heart failure

Political Party: Democratic-Republican

Wife: Ann Gerry

Careers: 5th vice president of the United States, 9th governor of Massachusetts, Massachusetts congressman

Religion: Episcopalian

Nicknames: The Soldier's Friend

Memorable Quote About Him: "If every Man here was a Gerry, the Liberties of America would be safe against the Gates of Earth and Hell."—John Adams

Founding Documents Signed: The Articles of Confederation and the Declaration of Independence[156]

BOOKS TO READ FOR MORE INFORMATION:
- *Life of Elbridge Gerry* by James Austin
- *Elbridge Gerry: Founding Father and Republican Statesman* by George Billias
- *Elbridge Gerry, Marblehead's Forgotten Son* by Robert Goodwin
- *The Rise and Development of the Gerrymander* by Elmer Griffith

16 Things You Never Knew About Elbridge Gerry

260. Elbridge Gerry entered Harvard at the age of 14 and graduated from there with a master's degree at the age of 20.

261. Elbridge Gerry is the Founder we can thank for the term "gerrymandering," which seems to be in the news quite a lot these days. Around 1813, when Gerry was Governor of Massachusetts, he supported and passed a redistricting bill that would ensure Democratic/Republican (they were one party then, up against the Federalists) control of the state Senate. The new district looked like a salamander, so his opponents came up with the term "gerrymander" to mock him and call attention to his blatant attempt to circumvent the legitimate electoral process.

262. In 1773, Elbridge Gerry, as part of his work on the Committee of Correspondence, helped establish a clinic on Cat Island, Marblehead where people could be inoculated against smallpox. And since ignorance breeds fear, and fear breeds violence, it wasn't long before mobs attacked the place and destroyed it. Why? Because they were afraid that the hospital would spread the disease rather than prevent it. The means of infection was still unknown so, of course, let's destroy what we don't understand. Gerry resigned the committee.

263. Elbridge Gerry was James Madison's vice president.

264. The Three-Fifths Compromise debated at the Constitutional Convention counted slaves as 3/5 of a person for reasons of Congressional apportionment. Gerry was adamantly opposed because it would have given Southern slaveholders a majority position in the House.

265. Elbridge Gerry was riding in a carriage on his way to the Senate when he collapsed and died, probably from a stroke.

266. Elbridge Gerry's tombstone reads, "The Only Signer of the Declaration of Independence Interred in Washington, D.C." His wife Ann is buried in New Haven, Connecticut.

267. Elbridge Gerry is in John Trumbull's iconic painting, *Declaration of Independence*. It appears on the back of the $2 bill.

Speaking Words of Wisdom . . .

268. "No religious doctrine shall be established by law."[157]

Militias prevent Armies?

269. "What, sir, is the use of a militia? It is to prevent the establishment of a standing army, the bane of liberty . . . Whenever governments mean to invade the rights and liberties of the people, they always attempt to destroy the militia, in order to raise an army upon their ruins."[158]

270. "The evils we experience flow from the excess of democracy. The people do not want virtue, but are the dupes of pretended patriots."[159]

271. "A standing army is like a standing member. It's an excellent assurance of domestic tranquility, but a dangerous temptation to foreign adventure."[160]

Advising caution . . .

272. "I am exceedingly distressed at the proceedings of the Convention-being . . . almost sure, they will . . . lay the foundation of a Civil War."[161]

Some orders should not be followed . . .

273. "Should We consent to an order of Cincinnati consisting of all the Officers of the Army & Citizens of Consiquence in the united States; how easy the Transition from a Republican to any other Form of Government, however despotic! & how rediculous to exchange a british Administration, for one that would be equally tyrannical, perhaps much more so? this project may answer the End of Courts that aim at making Us subservient to their political purposes, but can never be consistent with the Dignity or Happiness of the united States.—"[162]

What do atheists know anyway?

274. "The great object of our political Enterprize with Britain is obtained; & if We have Wisdom & Virtue to improve the advantages, the Issue must

be happy. 'Laus Deo' should be the Motto of America & inscribed on every Device for commemorating this great Event; for none but atheists can be insensible of the first obligations wch. result on the Occasion." [163]

Fighting for the Declaration . . .

275. "I have been fully employed since Thursday Noon in obtaining some Knowledge of the State of the Army and conferring with the different Corps of Officers from the General to the Field officers, and have the pleasure to inform You that they appear to be in high Spirits for Action and agree in Sentiments that the Men's as firm and determined as they wish them to be, having in View since the Declaration of Independence an object that they are ready to contend for, an object that they will chearfully pursue at the Risque of Life and every valuable Enjoyment." [164]

FOUNDERS WHO DID NOT SIGN THE UNITED STATES CONSTITUTION

Of the 70 delegates appointed to the Constitutional Convention, only 55 attended and, of those 55, only 39 signed the document.

The ones who did not attend had a variety of reasons, ranging from illness, to a dissatisfaction with the final draft—the primary reason being the lack of a Bill of Rights—to wanting to stay home and work. John Pickering, for example, wanted to expand his roster of law clients and develop his practice. Food on the table was more important that signature on a document, apparently.

Here is a list of the 30 Founders who did not sign the United States Constitution, for one reason or another.

- Charles Carroll
- Abraham Clark
- Francis Dana
- William Davie
- Gabriel Duvall
- Oliver Ellsworth
- Elbridge Gerry
- Robert Hanson Harrison
- Patrick Henry
- William Houston

- William Houstoun
- Thomas Jefferson
- John Lansing
- Henry Lauren
- Richard Henry Lee
- Luther Martin
- Alexander Martin
- George Mason
- James McClurg
- John Mercer
- Thomas Nelson

- Nathaniel Pendelton
- John Pickering
- William Pierce
- Edmund Randolph
- Thomas Stone
- Caleb Strong
- George Walton
- Erastus Wolcott
- George Wythe
- Robert Yates

CHAPTER 17
FRANCIS HOPKINSON

Don't Call Me Frances

If my poor abilities can be of the least service to my country in her day of trial I shall not complain of the hardship of the task.

BORN: September 21, 1737 in Philadelphia, Pennsylvania

DIED: May 9, 1791 in Philadelphia, Pennsylvania

AGE AT DEATH: 53

CAUSE OF DEATH: Epileptic seizure

POLITICAL PARTY: Federalist Party

WIFE: Ann Borden

CAREERS: Judge of the United States District Court for the District of Pennsylvania, delegate from New Jersey to the Second Constitutional Convention

RELIGION: Episcopalian

NICKNAMES: None

MEMORABLE QUOTE ABOUT HIM: "I received your kind Letter of the 22d Octr. last, which gave me great Pleasure as it inform'd me of your Welfare, and of your Appointment to the honourable Office of Treasurer of Loans. I think the Congress judg'd rightly in their Choice. An Exactness in Accounts, and scrupulous Fidelity in Matters of Trust, are Qualities for which your Father was eminent, and which I was persuaded were inherited by his Son when I took the Liberty of naming you one of the Executors of my Will, a Liberty which I hope you will excuse."—Benjamin Franklin[165]

FOUNDING DOCUMENT SIGNED: Declaration of Independence

BOOKS TO READ FOR MORE INFORMATION:
- *Francis Hopkinson, Musician, Poet and Patriot, 1737-1937* by Otto E Albrecht
- *The Life and Works of Francis Hopkinson* by George E. Hastings
- *The Flag Myth Involving Francis Hopkinson* by Ratcliffe M. Hills
- *Francis Hopkinson : The First American Poet-Composer and Our Musical Life In Colonial Times* by O. G. Sonneck

9 Things You Never Knew About Francis Hopkinson

276. Francis Hopkinson is credited as the designer of the American flag. Yes, even though many people still believe that Betsy Ross designed the flag, it was Frances Hopkinson who was the true designer and the journals of the Continental Congress provide written evidence of this claim.

277. As "Peter Grievous," Francis Hopkinson wrote a political satire of King George called, "A Pretty Story Written in the Year of Our Lord 1774." (The complete allegory is available online.)

278. Francis Hopkinson learned to play the harpsichord at the age of 17 and become so good at it, he regularly played with professional orchestras.

279. Francis Hopkinson wrote a number of songs, most of which were either about politics or religion. These are the lyrics of what is considered the first American secular song, "My Days Have Been So Wondrous Free." Music by Francis Hopkinson; lyrics by Thomas Parnell:

> My days have been so wondrous free,
> The little Birds that fly
> With careless Ease from Tree to Tree,
> Were but as blest as I,
> Were but as blest as I.
> Ask the gliding waters,
> If a Tear of mine
> Increas'd their Stream,
> And ask the breathing Gales
> If e'er I lent a Sigh to them,
> If I lent a Sigh to them.

You can hear the song performed by Thomas Hampson as part of the New York Philharmonic's Offstage atyoutube.com/watch?v=EtWgFU52uwM

280. Francis Hopkinson is the inventor of the Bellarmonic, a modification of the glass harmonica. The sounds it made used metal balls to create tones that sounded like bells. On June 28, 1786, Hopkinson wrote of his instrument in a letter to Thomas Jefferson:

> My spare Time and Attention is at present much engaged in a Project to make the Harmonica or musical Glasses to be played with Kees, like an Organ. I am now far forward in this Scheme and have little Doubt of Success. It has in vain been attempted in France and England. It may therefore seem too adventurous in me to undertake it, but the Door of Experiment is open; in Case of Disappointment the Projector is the only Sufferer.

On December 23, 1786, Jefferson replied to Hopkinson:

> I am very much pleased with your project on the Harmonica, & the prospect of your succeeding in the application of Keys to it. It will be the greatest present which has been made to the musical world this century, not excepting the Piano-forte. If its tone approaches that given by the finger as nearly only as he harpsichord does that of the harp, it will be very valuable . . .

281. Francis Hopkinson was a member of the first class to graduate from the University of Pennsylvania.

Speaking Words of Wisdom . . .

282. "When men of fortune turn common soldiers to fight for their liberties against the hand of oppression, success, I think, must attend their honest efforts, the tool of tyrannic power must shrink from before them." (1776)

It's in writing for a reason . . .

283. "It is so natural to expect some declaration of the will of contracting parties, when circumstances out of the reach of either have occurred,

which totally alters the principles upon which the contract was formed, that an omission of such declaration can have no other interpretation, but that of willful neglect or deep design, neither of which is the law disposed to countenance. Hence, probably, arose the custom of protest, in cafes of wreck, illegal capture, fire, and other unforseen and unavoidable accidents."[166]

Singing for freedom . . .

284. "Twas nobly done, to lend thy voice,
And soft harmonious song,
When Freedom was the rapturous theme
That warbled from thy tongue."[167]

THE MUSIC & POETRY OF FRANCIS HOPKINSON

A great number of the Founders were, of course, writers. And some wrote poetry. But Francis Hopkinson is the only Founder who had a significant discography of songs, as well as a bibliography of poems. Here is a list of his lyrical work.

Songs

- "Beneath A Weeping Willow's Shade"
- "Come Fair Rosina"
- "My Days Have Been So Wondrous Free"
- "My Love Is Gone To Sea"
- "Whilst Through The Sharp Hawthorne"

Poems

- "Rondo"
- "The Garland"
- "Give Me Thy Heart"
- "Song"
- "Advice to Amanda"
- "To Celia On Her Wedding Day"
- "Disappointed Love"
- "To Rosalinda On Her Birth Day"
- "To Myrtilla"
- "To Delia, Wrote On A Leaf In Her Pocket–Book"
- "Enraptur'd I Gaze When My Delia Is By"
- "See Down Maria's Blushing Cheek"
- "My Gen'rous Heart Disdains"

CHAPTER 18
RUFUS KING

Son of a Sea Captain

I never liked the Hierarchy of the Church . . .[168]

BORN: Match 24, 1755 in Scarborough, Massachusetts

DIED: April 29, 1827 in Jamaica, Queens, New York

AGE AT DEATH: 72

CAUSE OF DEATH: Unknown. A year before his death, he resigned his post of Minister Plenipotentiary in London and returned to New York due to "poor health."

POLITICAL PARTY: Federalist Party

WIFE: Mary Alsop King

CAREERS: Lawyer, investor, United States senator from New York, United States minister to Great Britain

RELIGION: Episcopalian

NICKNAMES: None

MEMORABLE QUOTES ABOUT HIM: "I am engaged in a famous Cause: The Cause of King, of Scarborough vs. a Mob, that broke into [Rufus King's] House, and rifled his Papers, and terrified him, his Wife, Children and Servants in the Night. The Terror, and Distress, the Distraction and Horror of this Family cannot be described by Words or painted upon Canvass. It is enough to move a Statue, to melt an Heart of Stone, to read the Story. It was not surprising that Richard King became a loyalist. All of his sons, however, became patriots in the American War of Independence."[169]

"Your conduct here has been so entirely proper, both as it has regarded the interest of your own Country and of this, as to have given me perfect satisfaction."[170]

"Mr. King is a man much distinguished for his eloquence and his parliamentary talents . . . .He may with propriety be ranked among the Luminaries of the present Age."[171]

FOUNDING DOCUMENT SIGNED: The United States Constitution

BOOKS TO READ FOR MORE INFORMATION:
- *Rufus King: American Federalist* by Robert Ernst
- *The Life and Correspondence of Rufus King, 1893–1897* (4 vol.) by Charles R. King
- *Rufus King and His Times* by Edward Hale Brush

10 Things You Never Knew About Rufus King

285. Rufus King's parents were wealthy. When the Stamp Act was passed in 1765, King's neighbors broke into the King house and trashed all the furniture. Later, their barn was burned down. Why did this happen to them? It was probably due to resentment over the taxes levied by the Stamp Act. But what does that have to do with the Kings? Nothing, except for the fact that the neighbors knew the tax wouldn't affect the Kings, so they took out their rage on the "1%" people of the time.

286. Rufus King was smart. How smart? He was first in his Harvard graduating class of 1777.

287. Rufus King's wife Mary Alsop, who he married when she was 16, was apparently quite beautiful. Massachusetts Congressman George Thatcher once said of her, "She is vastly the best looking woman I have seen since I have been in this city."

288. When Rufus King and his family lived in their mansion in Jamaica, New York, his account book showed that he paid a blacksmith, carpenter, wheelwright, harness maker, carriage maker, plasterer, well digger, spectacle maker, shoemaker, chimney sweep, millers, masons, cabinetmakers, and tailors.

289. It's hard to say "no" to the president. In 1825, Rufus King retired from the Senate because he was sick, although it was usually described back then as "being in ill health." We don't know what was wrong with him, but it was likely some kind of heart disease or chronic, fatal disease. Even though he certainly knew why King had retired, President John

Quincy Adams nonetheless asked him to serve as minister to Great Britain. As noted, it is extremely difficult to say "no" to a president when he or she asks you to serve, so King took the job. He didn't last very long, however, and returned to America, deferring to his health. He died 2 years later.

290. Rufus King's brother Cyrus was also a politician and held something of a record in the House of Representatives from 1813-1817. He only missed 54 of 465 roll call votes, which is 11.6 percent. This is quite better than the mean of 16.8 percent for all other representatives.

Speaking Words of Wisdom . . .

He probably slept in on Sundays . . .

291. "I never liked the Hierarchy of the Church—an equality in the teacher of Religion, and a dependence on the people, are republican sentiments—but if the clergy combine, they will have their influence on Government."[172]

Henry, the money sucks, but could you do it anyway?

292. "In fact; when congress shall be convinced by a particular statement of expenditure that the salary [for Secretary of War] is insufficient, they certainly will not refuse to increase it: the present sum therefore I hope will not be an objection."[173]

The Constitution is a must . . .

293. "The States under the [confederacy] are not sovereign States. They can do no act but such as are of a subordinate nature or such as terminate in themselves-and even these are restrained: coinage, [Public] office, etc. They are wholly incompetent to the exercise of any of the [great] & distinguishing acts of sovereignty. They can neither make nor receive embassies to or from any other sovereign. They have not the powers of injuring another or of defending themselves from an injury offered from one another. They are deaf, dumb and impotent."[174]

It took a while for the country to catch up with Rufus . . .

294. "I have yet to learn that one man can make a slave of another. If one man cannot do so, no number of individuals can have any better right to do it."[175]

CHAPTER 19
RICHARD HENRY LEE

Don't Call Me Dick

That these united Colonies are, and of right ought to be, free and independent States, that they are absolved from all allegiance from the British crown, and that all political connection between America and the State of Great Britain is, and ought to be, totally dissolved . . .[176]

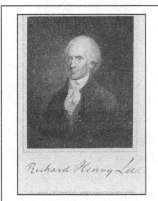

BORN: January 20, 1732 in Westmoreland County, Virginia

DIED: June 19, 1794 in Westmoreland County, Virginia

AGE AT DEATH: 62

CAUSE OF DEATH: Unknown. All we know is that he died at home. Heart failure or stroke seem likely contenders for the cause, though.

POLITICAL PARTY: Anti-Administration

WIVES: Anne Aylett; Anne (Gaskins) Pinckard

CAREERS: Senator from Virginia, 2nd president *pro tempore* of the United States Senate, 12th president of the Continental Congress

RELIGION: Episcopalian

MEMORABLE QUOTE ABOUT HIM: "Richard Henry Lee aided in lighting the torch of American Freedom and kept it burning for his nation. From a farmer, to a politician, to congressman, to a statesman, to a patriot, to a senator, Richard Henry Lee performed a very important role in American history."[177]

"Richard Henry Lee, tall and spare, is a deep thinker, and a masterly man, able and inflexible, a scholar, a gentleman, and of uncommon eloquence."[178]

FOUNDING DOCUMENTS SIGNED: The Articles of Confederation, the United States Constitution

BOOKS TO READ FOR MORE INFORMATION:
- *Richard Henry Lee of Virginia: A Portrait of an American Revolutionary* by J. Kent McGaughy
- *Richard Henry Lee, Statesman of the Revolution* by Oliver Perry Chitwood
- *Richard Henry Lee* by John Carter Matthews
- *The Letters of Richard Henry Lee* by Richard Henry Lee and James Curtis Ballagh

11 Things You Never Knew About Richard Henry Lee

295. Richard Henry Lee was born in Virginia, but because his family could afford it, and because the quality of education in England was believed to be superior to that in America (it was), he was sent to a school in Wakesfield, Yorkshire, England for his primary education. He excelled.

296. Richard Henry Lee was an active participant in the First Continental Congress and was, it was widely agreed, a superb speaker. Many witnesses compared his speaking prowess with that of Cicero.

297. Richard Henry Lee was so convinced of the supreme necessity and importance of the sovereignty of states that he wanted Virginia to secede from the Union if the Bill of Rights was not ratified.

298. Richard Henry Lee was worried about the Constitution. He opined that it had "a strong tendency to aristocracy." (Patrick Henry had previously said that he felt the Constitution "squints toward monarchy." These guys were concerned about making the grievous mistake of creating an American "kingdom," thus bringing to the New World everything the colonists sought to avoid by declaring independence from the British kingdom.)

299. Richard Henry Lee was the great-uncle of Robert E. Lee.

300. Richard Henry Lee worried that the United States Constitution would lead to a civil war.

Speaking Words of Wisdom . . .

Watch whom you give power to . . .

301. "There are certain unalienable and fundamental rights, which inform-
ing the social compact, out to be explicitly ascertained and fixed, a
free and enlightened people, in forming this compact, will not resign
all their rights to those who govern, and they will fix limits to their
legislators and rulers, which will soon be plainly seen by those who
are governed, as well as by those who govern: and the latter will know
they cannot be passed unperceived by the former, and without giving a
general alarm."[179]

Did you hear me? Watch who you give power to?

302. "And what country can preserve its liberties, if its rulers are not warned
from time to time, that this people preserve the spirit of resistance? Let
them take arms. The remedy is to set them right as to the facts, pardon
and pacify them. What signify a few lives lost in a century or two? The
tree of liberty must be refreshed from time to time, with the blood of
patriots and tyrants. It is its natural manure."[180]

Yeah . . . why not?

303. "It is true, we are not disposed to differ much, at present, about religion; but when we are making a constitution, it is to be hoped, for ages
and millions yet unborn, why not establish the free exercise of religion
as a part of the national compact." [181]

We shall be free . . .

304. "The good people of the United States in their late generous contest,
contended for free government in the fullest, clearest, and strongest
sense. that they had not idea of being brought under despotic rule
under the notion of Strong Government, or in the form of elective despotism: Chains being still Chains, whether made of gold or
iron. The corrupting nature of power, and its insatiable appetite for
increase."[182]

Not crazy about you using the word "asylum" there, Dick . . .

305. "Why then sir, why do we longer delay? Why still deliberate? Let this happy day give birth to an American Republic. Let her arise not to devastate and to conquer but to reestablish the reign of peace and law. The eyes of Europe are fixed upon us. She demands of us a living example of freedom that may exhibit a contrast in the felicity of the citizen to the ever-increasing tyranny which desolates her polluted shores. She invites us to prepare an asylum where the unhappy may find solace, and the persecuted repose. If we are not this day wanting in our duty, the names of the American legislators of 1776 will be placed by posterity at the side of all of those whose memory has been and ever will be dear to virtuous men and good citizens."[183]

Favorite Drinks of the Founding Fathers

The Founders could imbibe. Boy, could they imbibe. This is a list of some of the favorite beverages of 5 of our favorite Founders.

George Washington: Wine and whiskey
Washington had a very successful distillery at Mount Vernon which is still brewing to this day.

John Adams: Hard cider, Madeira wine with rum
John Adams started his days at Harvard with beer and bread. The inclusion of alcohol throughout his day continued throughout his life.

Thomas Jefferson: Wine
Thomas Jefferson was a big-time oenophile.

Benjamin Franklin: Beer and wine
Franklin so loved his wine he once said, "Behold the rain which descends from heaven upon our vineyards, there it enters the roots of the vines, to be changed into wine, a constant proof that God loves us, and loves to see us happy."

Samuel Adams: Beer
He was a brewer, and a company named their beer after him.

CHAPTER 20
ROBERT R. LIVINGSTON

"Place Your Hand . . ."

The noblest work of our whole lives . . .

BORN: November 27, 1746 in New York City, New York

DIED: February 26, 1813 in Clermont, New York

AGE AT DEATH: 66

CAUSE OF DEATH: Multiple strokes that eventually killed him.

POLITICAL PARTY: Democratic-Republican

WIFE: Mary Stevens

CAREERS: Lawyer, United States minister to France, 1st United States secretary of foreign affairs, 1st chancellor of New York

NICKNAME: The Chancellor

FOUNDING DOCUMENTS SIGNED: None.

BOOKS TO READ FOR MORE INFORMATION:
- *An American Aristocracy: The Livingstons* by Clare Brandt
- *Negotiating the Louisiana Purchase: Robert Livingston's Mission to France, 1801-1804* by Frank W. Brecher
- *Chancellor Robert R. Livingston of New York, 1746-1813* by George Dangerfield

14 Things You Never Knew About Robert R. Livingston

306. Robert R. Livingston administered the presidential oath of office to George Washington.

307. Robert R. Livingston and Robert Fulton once had a deal to build a commercially successful steamboat. One of their first tries sank in the Seine.

308. In 1776, Robert R. Livingston, along with Thomas Jefferson, Benjamin Franklin, John Adams, and Roger Sherman—the Committee of Five— worked on drafting the Declaration of Independence. Livingston left the Second Continental Congress before he had a chance to sign it.

309. In 1773, Livingston was appointed recorder of the City of New York. He was fired for speaking out against England and in support of the colonies.

310. Livingston was very wealthy, and when he built his home in Clermont, New York, he outfitted with the finest, well, of everything. The word spread and it wasn't long before his mansion, first called "New Clermont," and then "Arryl" (a phonetic spelling of his three initials), it became known as "the most commodious home in America."

311. Arryl had a library of over 4,000 volumes.

312. It is believed that Livingston and his family owned close to 1,000,000 acres of land.

313. Livingston, as United States minister to France, once criticized John Adams in way that pissed Adams off to no end. Adams was in the Netherlands negotiating a loan for the States. He was doing well, and he garnered favorable terms, but Livingston sent him a letter accusing him of a "ridiculous display" of self-aggrandizing vanity in front of the Dutch Court. This infuriated Adams, who was especially sensitive to being called vain. (Probably because he was.) Vehement correspondence ensued.

314. One of Robert R. Livingston's agricultural passions was the breeding of Merino sheep.

Speaking Words of Wisdom . . .

We're Number 1! We're Number 1!

315. "We have lived long but this is the noblest work of our whole lives . . . The United States take rank this day among the first powers of the world."[184]

We know we'll win, too . . .

316. "On the whole I think it would be more dignified and more safe to act upon our ground and if we must enter into the war [against Napoleon], secure to ourselves all the advantages that may result from [doing so]."[185]

Sincerest condolences . . . on a truly stupid death . . .

317. "I sincerely lament with you the death of young Hamilton and the more in that it originated in the unhappy party spirit which has too long disturbed the peace of our societies."[186]

Regarding the Louisiana territory . . .

318. "My views of the importance of Louisiana are exactly similar to yours and they lead me more and more to regret the loss of that treaty which secured it from ever passing into the hands of France." [187]

You can't win if you don't play . . .

319. "I beg the favor that you purchase for me a ticket in the State Lottery and retain it in your hands transmitting me the number." [188]

Visiting the Founding Fathers

This is a list of places to visit pertaining to some of the Founding Fathers discussed in this volume. These places are either homes, museums, national park sites, or locations. (For example, Sam Adams's only destination is a plaque.) Always do your research and plan ahead before visiting one of these places.

George Washington
George Washington's Mount Vernon
Mount Vernon, Virginia

Thomas Jefferson
Monticello
Charlottesville, Virginia

Alexander Hamilton
Hamilton Grange National Memorial
St. Nicholas Park
New York City, New York

John Adams
Adams National Historical Park
Quincy, Massachusetts

Benjamin Franklin

Benjamin Franklin Museum
Philadelphia, Pennsylvania

James Madison

Montpelier
Orange, Virginia

John Jay

John Jay Homestead State Historic Site
Katonah, New York

James Monroe

Ash Lawn–Highland
Charlottesville, Virginia

Thomas Paine

Thomas Paine Cottage
New Rochelle, New York

Patrick Henry

Scotchtown
Hanover County, Virginia

Samuel Adams

Sam Adams Home (site plaque only)
24 Winter Street
Boston, Massachusetts

John Hancock

Hancock–Clarke House
Lexington, Massachusetts

William Blount

William Blount Mansion
Knoxville, Tennessee

Charles Carroll of Carrollton

Charles Carroll House
Annapolis, Maryland

John Dickinson

John Dickinson House
Dover, Delaware

Elbridge Gerry

Elbridge Gerry House
Marblehead, Massachusetts

Francis Hopkinson

Francis Hopkinson House
Bordentown, New Jersey

Rufus King

King Manor
Jamaica, Queens, New York

Richard Henry Lee

Francis and Richard Henry Lee House
Montross, Virginia

Robert R. Livingston

The Chancellor Robert R Livingston
Masonic Library
New York, New York

John Marshall

John Marshall House
Richmond, Virginia

Rufus King

Gunston Hall
Mason Neck, Virginia

Gouverneur Morris

Gouverneur Museum
Gouverneur, New York

Charles Cotesworth Pinckney

Charles Pinckney
Charles Pinckney National Historic Site
Mount Pleasant, South Carolina

Benjamin Rush

Benjamin Rush House
Chester County, Pennsylvania

Roger Sherman

Northrup House Museum
Sherman, Connecticut

John Witherspoon

The President's House
Princeton, New Jersey

George Wythe

Wythe House
Williamsburg, Virginia

CHAPTER 21
JOHN MARSHALL

The Marshall Who Was a Captain

The power to tax is the power to destroy.[189]

BORN: September 24, 1755 in Germantown, Virginia

DIED: July 6, 1835 in Philadelphia, Pennsylvania

AGE AT DEATH: 79

CAUSE OF DEATH: Unknown. He suffered from bladder stones and was successfully treated for them. He experienced declining health, however, after his wife died, and he died a year later.

POLITICAL PARTY: Federalist Party

WIFE: Mary "Polly" Willis Ambler

CAREERS: Fourth chief justice of the Supreme Court, 4th United States secretary of state, member of the United States House of Representatives for Virginia.

RELIGION: Episcopalian

NICKNAME: The Great Chief Justice

MEMORABLE QUOTE ABOUT HIM: "No one admires more than I do the extraordinary powers of Marshall's mind; no one respects more his amiable deportment in private life. He is the most unpretending and unassuming of men. His abilities and his virtues render him an ornament not only to Virginia, but to our nature."[190]

FOUNDING DOCUMENT SIGNED: Articles of Confederation

BOOKS TO READ FOR MORE INFORMATION:
- *John Marshall: A Life in Law* by Leonard Baker
- *The Life of John Marshall* (4 vols.) by Albert J. Beveridge
- *John Marshall and the Constitution: A Chronicle of the Supreme Court* by Edward Samuel Corwin
- *The Great Chief Justice: John Marshall and the Rule of Law* by Charles Hobson
- *The Chief Justiceship of John Marshall from 1801 to 1835* by Herbert A. Johnson
- *John Marshall and the Heroic Age of the Supreme Court* by R. Kent Newmyer
- *John Marshall and InternationalLaw: Statesman, and Chief Justice* by Frances H. Rudko
- *What Kind of Nation: Thomas Jefferson, John Marshall, and the Epic Struggle to Create a United States* by James F. Simon
- *John Marshall: Definer Of A Nation* by Jean Edward Smith
- *John Marshall: Defender of the Constitution* by Francis N. Stites
- *John Marshall, The Chief Justice Who Saved the Nation* by Harlow Giles Unger

17 Things You Never Knew About John Marshall

320. John Marshall served 12,570 days as Chief Justice of the United States Supreme Court, from February 4, 1801 until July 6, 1835, and to this day he remains the longest serving chief justice in Supreme Court history.

321. John Marshall was a graduate of the College of William & Mary.

322. We owe enormous thanks to John Marshall, especially in these days of radical, fundamentalist, often religious-based laws being passed in (too many) states. It was Chief Justice Marshall who established that the Supreme Court could strike down state laws that violated the Constitution. Many, many bad state laws have been judged unconstitutional and abrogated thanks to Marshall's wisdom and foresight.

323. John Marshall was President John Adams' Secretary of State before being made Supreme Court Chief Justice.

324. John Marshall was a captain in the Culpeper Militiamen, a militia group formed in 1775 in the area around Culpeper, Virginia. They fought for the American revolutionaries as needed.

325. John Marshall and his wife Mary Willis Ambler had 10 children.

326. John Marshall was born in a log cabin in Virginia in 1755.

327. Thomas Jefferson was related to John Marshall on his mother's side. They were both descendants of William Randolph, an English-born colonist of Virginia, who was known, along with his wife, Mary Isham, as the "Adam and Eve of Virginia." (Lots of prominent people were descendants or relatives of Randolph.)

Speaking Words of Wisdom . . .

Word . . .

328. "To listen well is as powerful a means of communication and influence as to talk well."

The gavel rules . . .

329. "It is emphatically the province and duty of the judicial department to say what the law is. If two laws conflict with each other, the courts must decide on the operation of each. This is of the very essence of judicial duty."[191]

No such thing as activist judges . . .

330. "Courts are the mere instruments of the law, and can will nothing. When they are said to exercise a discretion, it is a mere legal discretion, a discretion to be exercised in discerning the course prescribed by law; and, when that is discerned, it is the duty of the Court to follow it. Judicial power is never exercised for the purpose of giving effect to the will of the Judge; always for the purpose of giving effect to the will of the Legislature; or, in other words, to the will of the law.[192]

On the Constitution

331. "The Constitution is not a panacea for every blot upon the public welfare, nor should this Court, ordained as a judicial body, be thought of as a general haven for reform movements."

332. "The people made the Constitution, and the people can unmake it. It is the creature of their own will, and lives only by their will."[193]

333. "Let the end be legitimate, let it be within the scope of the constitution, and all means which are appropriate, which are plainly adapted to that end, which are not prohibited, but consist with the letter and spirit of the constitution, are constitutional."[194]

334. "No political dreamer was ever wild enough to think of breaking down the lines which separate the States, and of compounding the American people into one common mass. Of consequence, when they act, they act in their States. But the measures they adopt do not, on that account, cease to be the measures of the people themselves, or become the measures of the State governments. From these conventions the Constitution derives its whole authority. The government proceeds directly from the people; is 'ordained and established' in the name of the people, and is declared to be ordained, 'in order to form a more perfect union, establish justice, insure domestic tranquillity, and secure the blessings of liberty to themselves and to their posterity'."[195]

Innocent until . . .

335. "The law does not expect a man to be prepared to defend every act of his life which may be suddenly and without notice alleged against him."[196]

Divided between . . .

336. "In America, the powers of sovereignty are divided between the Government of the Union and those of the States. They are each sovereign with respect to the objects committed to it, and neither sovereign with respect to the objects committed to the other. We cannot comprehend that train of reasoning, which would maintain that the extent of power granted by the people is to be ascertained not by the nature and terms of the grant, but by its date. Some State Constitutions were formed before, some since, that of the United States. We cannot believe that their relation to each other is in any degree dependent upon this circumstance. Their respective powers must, we think, be precisely the same as if they had been formed at the same time."[197]

CHAPTER 22
GEORGE MASON

The Mason Who Wasn't a Mason

As much as I value an union of all the states, I would not admit the southern states into the union, unless they agreed to the discontinuance of this disgraceful trade, because it would bring weakness and not strength to the union.[198]

BORN: December 11, 1725 in Fairfax County, Virginia

DIED: October 7, 1792 in Fairfax County, Virginia

AGE AT DEATH: 66

CAUSE OF DEATH: Probably pneumonia from an epidemic of respiratory illnesses that made their way through Gunston Hall in Virginia.

POLITICAL PARTY: Anti-Federalist Party

WIVES: Sarah Brent; Ann Eilbeck

CAREERS: Delegate to the U.S. Constitutional Convention of 1787, planter, political theorist

RELIGION: Anglican, Episcopalian

NICKNAMES: Father of the Bill of Rights

FOUNDING DOCUMENTS SIGNED: None. He refused to sign the United States Constitution because it did not contain a Bill of Rights.

BOOKS TO READ FOR MORE INFORMATION:
- *George Mason, Forgotten Founder* by Jeff Broadwater
- *The Five George Masons: Patriots and Planters of Virginia and Maryland* by Pamela C. Copeland and Richard K. MacMaster

- *The Quartet: Orchestrating the Second American Revolution, 1783-1789* by Joseph J. Ellis
- *George Mason and George Washington: The Power of Principle* by Gerard W. Gawalt
- *George Mason, Gentleman Revolutionary* by Helen Hill Miller
- *George Mason, Reluctant Statesman* by Robert Allen Rutland

14 Things You Never Knew About George Mason

337. George Mason is highly responsible for the existence and ratification of the Bill of Rights, although he is not as well-known for his achievements as he should be. In fact, he was the author of the 1776 Virginia Declaration of Rights which was described as a "Bill of Rights."

338. George Mason was against ratification of the U.S. Constitution. Why? Because as originally written, it did *not* include a Bill of Rights.

339. Even though he had no formal education, none other than Thomas Jefferson described George Mason as the "wisest man of his generation." Mason educated himself from his uncle John Mercer's library. Mercer was a lawyer and became Mason's guardian after Mason's father died in a sailing accident on the Potomac.

340. George Mason was ahead of his time in terms of his perception of politicians. He called them "babblers" and avoided them at all costs.

341. When building Gunston Hall, his plantation home, George Mason devised a formula for mortar that was specifically created to prevent an onslaught of "those pernicious little vermin, the cockroaches."[199]

342. Interestingly, George Mason was well-liked, even though he was what many people described as irritable and short-tempered. He was also a hypochondriac.

343. George Mason annoyed James Madison with his use of the word "toleration" in the Virginia Bill of Rights. (See the Mason quote below.) Madison felt that Mason was saying that freedom of conscience was a right that the government could bestow upon the citizens. His position was that freedom of religion was a natural right that no one could legislate, but he kept his mouth shut. He did later convince Mason to rewrite the clause.

344. When George Mason took over George Washington's seat in the Virginia Legislature, he was miserable, and almost fainted from his dismay.

He wrote to Washington, "I was never in so disagreeable a situation, and almost despaired of a cause which I saw so ill conducted. Mere vexation and disgust threw me into such an ill state of health that before the convention rose, I was sometimes near fainting in the House."[200]

Speaking Words of Wisdom . . .

No force, no violence? Nice plan if it works . . .

345. "That religion, or the duty which we owe to our Creator, and the manner of discharging it, can be directed only by reason and conviction, not by force or violence; and therefore all men are equally entitled to the free exercise of religion, according to the dictates of conscience; and that it is the mutual duty of all to practice Christian forebearance, love, and charity towards each other."[201]

Ditto . . .

346. "That religion . . . can be governed only by reason and conviction, not by force or violence, and, therefore, that all men should enjoy the fullest toleration in the exercise of religion, according to the dictates of conscience."[202]

Conscientious objection . . . to religion

347. "It is contrary to the principles of reason and justice that any should be compelled to contribute to the maintenance of a church with which their consciences will not permit them to join, and from which they can derive no benefit; for remedy whereof, and that equal liberty as well religious as civil, may be universally extended to all the good people of this commonwealth."[203]

We do not deny . . . for now

348. "We do not deny the supreme Authority of Great Britain over her Colonys, but it is a Power which a wise Legislature will exercise with extreme Tenderness & Caution, and carefully avoid the least Imputation or Suspicion of Partiality. Wou'd to God that this Distinction between us & your fellow Subjects residing in Great Britain, by depriving us of

the ancient Tryal, by a Jury of our Equals, and substituting in its place an arbitrary Civil Law Court."[204]

Keep your replies to yourself . . .

349. "If the Maxims have asserted, & the Reflections I have made, are in themselves just, they will need no Vindication; if they are erronious, I shall esteem it a Favour to have my Errors pointed out; and will, in modest Silence, kiss the Rod that corrects me."[205]

He's not called "Father of the Bill of Rights" for nothing . . .

350. "That all Men are born equally free and independant, and have certain inherent natural Rights, of which they can not by any Compact, deprive or divest their Posterity; among which are the Enjoyment of Life and Liberty, with the Means of acquiring and possessing Property, and pursueing and obtaining Happiness and Safety."[206]

GEORGE MASON WAS NOT A MASON:

13 SIGNERS OF THE CONSTITUTION WHO WERE FREEMASONS

There are many conspiracy theories about the role of freemasonry in the founding of America. The design of Washington, D.C. and the design of the $1 bill, for starters. Plus, what's a Rosicrucian and who are the Illuminati? And does the Yale secret society Skull & Bones have anything to do with all this?

Those questions are the province of another book, but interestingly, here is a list of 13 Founders who were Masons.

- Gunning Bedford Jr. (Delaware)
- John Blair (Virginia)
- David Brearley (New Jersey)
- Jacob Broom (Delaware)
- Daniel Carroll (Maryland)
- Jonathan Dayton (New Jersey)
- John Dickinson (Delaware)
- Benjamin Franklin (Pennsylvania)
- Nicholas Gilman (New Hampshire)
- Rufus King (Massachusetts)
- James McHenry (Maryland)
- William Paterson (New Jersey)
- George Washington (Virginia)

Chapter 23
Gouverneur Morris

That's Gouverneur, Not Governor

It is not easy to be wise for all times, not event for the present much less for the future; and those who judge the past must recollect that, when it was the present the present was future.[207]

GOVERNEER MORRIS E.SQ^R
Member of Congress

BORN: January 31, 1752 in New York City, New York

DIED: November 6, 1816 in New York City, New York

AGE AT DEATH: 64

CAUSE OF DEATH: Internal injuries he caused himself. He tried to clear a urinary blockage by inserting a piece of whale bone up his urethra. This caused a devastating infection and fatal internal injuries.

POLITICAL PARTY: Federalist Party

WIFE: Anne Cary "Nancy" Randolph

CAREERS: United States Senator, Delegate to the Constitutional Convention of 1787

RELIGION: Anglican/Episcopalian

NICKNAMES: Penman of the Constitution, the Eternal Speaker,[208] the Gentleman Revolutionary

MEMORABLE QUOTES ABOUT HIM: "Perhaps his greatest interest for us lies in the fact that he was a shrewder, more far-seeing observer and recorder of contemporary men and events, both at home and abroad, than any other American or foreign statesman of his time. But aside from this he did much lasting work. He took a most prominent part in bringing about the independence of the colonies, and afterwards in welding them into a single powerful nation, whose greatness he both foresaw and foretold. He made the final draft of the United States Constitution; he first outlined our present system of national coinage; he originated and got under way the plan for the Erie Canal; as minister to France he successfully performed the most difficult task ever allotted to an American representative at a foreign capital. With all his faults, there are few men of his generation to whom the country owes more than to Gouverneur Morris."—Theodore Roosevelt[209]

"He never would concur in upholding domestic slavery. It was a nefarious institution. It was the curse of heaven in the States where it prevailed."[210]

FOUNDING DOCUMENTS SIGNED: The Articles of Confederation, the United States Constitution*[211]

* Gouverneur Morris wrote large sections of the Constitution (especially the Preamble), but refused to sign it because he felt it did not directly guarantee the rights of U.S. citizens.

BOOKS TO READ FOR MORE INFORMATION:
- *Gouverneur Morris: An Independent Life* by William Howard Adams
- *Gentleman Revolutionary: Gouverneur Morris, the Rake Who Wrote the Constitution* by Richard Brookhiser
- *Gouverneur Morris: Author, Statesman, and Man of the World* by James J. Kirschke
- *Envoy to the Terror: Gouverneur Morris and the French Revolution* by Melanie Randolph Miller
- *The Diaries of Gouverneur Morris: European Travels, 1794-1798* by Gouverneur Morris and Melanie Randolph Miller
- *The Diary and Letters of Gouverneur Morris, Minister of the United States to France; Member of the Constitutional Convention*, 2 vols., edited by Anne Cary Morris
- *Gouverneur Morris* by Theodore Roosevelt
- *The Extraordinary Mr. Morris* by Howard Swiggert

Things You Never Knew About Gouverneur Morris

351. After the 1787 Continental Congress, Gouverneur Morris sailed to France, ended up staying for a decade, and ultimately made himself a fortune before returning to the U.S. in 1799.

352. Gouverneur Morris caught his leg in a wagon wheel in 1780. The leg was amputated and he wore a "peg leg" for the rest of his life.

353. Since Gouverneur Morris was known as the "Penman of the Constitution," it's not surprising that there were others in his family who were writers, most notably, his great grandson Gouverneur Morris IV. Gouv IV graduated from Yale and went on to write novels, short stories, and screenplays, including *When My Ship Comes In*, *The Penalty*, *Yellow Men and Gold*, *East of Java*, and "You Can't Get Away With It," all of which were adapted as movies.

354. Gouverneur Morris was a financial expert and he helped plan the U.S. decimal coinage system, which is the basis for the U.S. monetary system.

355. Gouverneur Morris was in charge of the construction of the Erie Canal.

356. Gouverneur Morris had a truly terrible death, and it was all his own doing. (To the gentlemen reading this: prepare your cringe reflex.) Morris had a urinary tract blockage. (You can probably already see where this is going, right?) In an attempt to clear the blockage, he jammed a piece of whale bone up his urethra, causing fatal internal injuries and a devastating infection. (Told ya.)

357. Gouverneur Morris once unwisely accepted a bet that resulted in none other than George Washington himself giving him what Jerry Seinfeld would call the "stink eye." Someone bet Morris a dinner that he wouldn't go up to Washington and slap him on the back as if they were old friends. He did it, Washington was not pleased, and Morris later admitted regretting taking the bet.

Speaking Words of Wisdom . . .

Damn straight . . .

358. "This magistrate is not the king. The people are the king."[212]

I'll work, but . . .

359. "In adopting a republican form of government, I not only took it as a man does his wife, for better or for worse, but what a few men do with

their wives, I took it knowing all of its bad qualities. Neither ingratitude, therefore, nor slander can disappoint expectation nor excite surprise. If, in arduous circumstances, the voice of my country should call for my services, and I have the well-founded belief, that they can be useful, they shall certainly be rendered, but I hope that no such circumstances will arise, and in the mean time, 'pleas'd let me trifle life away.'"[213]

Foresight . . .

360. "The Rich will strive to establish their dominion and enslave the rest. They always did. They always will. The proper security against them is to form them into a separate interest. The 2 forces will then control each other. Let the rich mix with the poor and in a Commercial Country, they will establish an oligarchy. Take away commerce, and the democracy will triumph. Thus it has been all the world over. So it will be among us. Reason tells us we are but men: and we are not to expect any particular interference of Heaven in our favor. By thus combining & setting apart, the aristocratic interest, the popular interest will be combined against it. There will be a mutual check and mutual security."[214]

Gouverneur Morris was a staunch advocate against slavery . . .

361. "Upon what principle is it that the slaves shall be computed in the representation? Are they men? Then make them citizens, and let them vote. Are they property? Why, then, is no other property included? The houses in this city are worth more than all the wretched slaves who cover the rice swamps of South Carolina. The admission of slaves into the Representation when fairly explained comes to this: that the inhabitant of Georgia and South Carolina who goes to the Coast of Africa, and in defiance of the most sacred laws of humanity tears away his fellow creatures from their dearest connections and damns them to the most cruel bondages, shall have more votes in a Government instituted for protection of the rights of mankind, than the Citizen of Pennsylvania or New Jersey who views with a laudable horror, so nefarious a practice."[215]

A eulogy for George Washington

362. "In him were the courage of a soldier, the intrepidity of a chief, the fortitude of a hero. He had given to the impulsions of bravery all the

calmness of his character, and, if in the moment of danger, his manner was distinguishable from that of common life, it was by superior ease and grace."[216]

The scourge of prejudice . . .

363. "There is therefore an essential Difference between Prejudice and Error. The latter always wrong in itself is nevertheless to be pardoned when proper Means have been used to discover Truth. The former, however it may be indulged can never in Strictness be justified and is then compleatly odious when it invades the Rights or Happiness of Individuals or of Society."[217]

The patriot

364. "The Love of our Country is a primal Sense—the fair Impression of that Hand which form'd the human Heart. And with the characteristic Simplicity of creative Wisdom it is intimately blended with and strengthened by every other virtuous and honorable Sentiment. It is interwoven with the Bonds of connubial Tenderness, hallowed by the pious Sense of filial Duty, endear'd by the Charities of parental affection, nourished by the social Habits of Life, animated by the Fellowships of Youth, confirmed by the Amities of Age, and consecrated by the Mysteries of Religion."[218]

Hear, hear . . .

365. "To levy Taxes by Quotas is pernicious."[219]

CHAPTER 24
ROBERT MORRIS

Morris in the Can

Taxation to a certain point is not only proper but useful, because by stimulating the industry of individuals it increases the wealth of the Community. But when Taxes go so far as to intrench on the subsistence of the people they become burdensome and oppressive.[220]

BORN: January 20, 1734 in Liverpool, England

DIED: May 8, 1806 in Philadelphia, Pennsylvania

AGE AT DEATH: 72

CAUSE OF DEATH: Unknown, but as was common, writings report he suffered from "deteriorating health."

POLITICAL PARTY: Pro-Administration

WIFE: Mary White Morris

CAREERS: Merchant, United States superintendent of finance, United States senator from Pennsylvania

RELIGION: Episcopalian

NICKNAMES: None

MEMORABLE QUOTES ABOUT HIM: "Robert Morris (Pennsylvania) is a merchant of great eminence and wealth; an able Financier, and a worthy Patriot. He has an understanding equal to any public object, and possesses an energy of mind that few Men can boast of. Although he is not learned, yet he is as great as those who are. I am told that when he speaks in the Assembly of Pennsylvania, that he bears down all before him."[221]

"There were people in Congress who through their whole careers considered Morris to be everything the Revolution was against. He was about commerce, he was about self-interest. There was an ideological divide within the revolutionaries from the very beginning. It was between the ideologues, who believed that we should set up a society based on ideas, that people should act a new way; and then there were pragmatists, Morris primary among them, who took self-interest into account. He believed that to expect people to act in any other way was naive."[222]

FOUNDING DOCUMENTS SIGNED: The Declaration of Independence, the Articles of Confederation, the United States Constitution

BOOKS TO READ FOR MORE INFORMATION:
- *The Papers of Robert Morris 1781–1784* (9 vols.) edited by E. James Ferguson
- *Robert Morris's Folly: The Architectural and Financial Failures of an American Founder* by Ryan K. Smith
- *Robert Morris, Revolutionary Financier* by Clarence L. Ver Steeg

12 Things You Never Knew About Robert Morris

366. It can justifiably be opined that Robert Morris—as did all of the Founders—lived in a mean-spirited time. After losing a fortune in bad land investments, he went bankrupt, which was not as relatively benign as it is today. Due to his financial problems, he ended up serving 3 years in a debtor's prison. Congress eventually passed a law freeing him, but it is true that a Founding Father and signer of the Declaration of Independence and the Constitution went to prison because he couldn't pay his debts.

367. Robert Morris's father, Robert Sr., died as a result of a ceremony to honor him. A ship's gun exploded and killed Robert Sr. at his own tribute event. His last thoughts probably encompassed something along the lines of, "Y'know, I could have done without being honored if this was going to be the price I'd pay."

368. Robert Morris was a slave trader. While in business with Thomas Willing, they funded the importation of slaves and even ran slave auctions.

369. In 1786, none other than George Washington wrote to Robert Morris. The gist of his letter? *I really hope democracy can bring an end to slavery.* (Big hint from the Commander in Chief, wouldn't you say?)

370. At first, Robert Morris was against independence. Why? Ever the pragmatist, Morris didn't think the colonists would win in a war with England.

371. In 1763, Robert Morris fathered a child out of wedlock. The mother is unknown; the baby was named Mary but, was known as Polly. Morris supported her and she married at age 18. They were apparently on good terms throughout his life.

372. Robert Morris was a pre-capitalism global capitalist. And he made a fortune in trading. Biographer Charles Rappleye notes that Morris was "very much a free market, *laissez-faire* capitalist—he talked about trade being as free as the air."[223]

373. During the Revolutionary War, George Washington wrote to Robert Morris to ask him for the sum of $10,000, professing that he needed it immediately. Morris didn't have it, but borrowed it from a Quaker friend who lent it to him based solely on Morris's word. "Sir, you must let me have it." Morris said. "My note and my honour will be your only security." The Quaker immediately gave him the money. Morris's actions kept Washington's army stocked in gunpowder, as well as clothing, for that matter.

Speaking Words of Wisdom . . .

A necessary evil . . .

374. "In every Society also there must be some Taxes, because the necessity of supporting Government & defending the State always exist. To do these on the cheapest Terms is wise, and when it is considered how much men are disposed to indolence and profusion it will appear that (even if those demands did not require the whole of what could be raised) still it would be wise to carry Taxation to a certain amount, and expend what should remain after providing for the support of Government and the National defense in Works of public utility, such as opening of roads and Navigation."[224]

A necessary evil, continued . . .

375. "For Taxes operate two ways towards the increase of National Wealth. First they stimulate industry to provide the means of payment, secondly they encourage economy so far as to avoid the purchase of unnecessary things and keep money in readiness for the Tax gatherer."[225]

Yet people still drink, Bob . . .

376. "It may be boldly affirmed, that no inconvenience can arise from laying a heavy tax on the use of ardent spirits. These have always been equally prejudicial to the constitutions and morals of the people."[226]

Religion may help, but justice is inherent . . .

377. "I need no inspiration to show that justice establishes a nation. Neither are the principles of religion necessary to evince that political injustice will receive political chastisement. Religious men will cherish these maxims in proportion to the additional force they derive from divine revelation."[227]

CHAPTER 25
WILLIAM PATERSON

Here Come Da Judge

Look well to the characters and qualifications of those you elect and raise to office and places of trust.[228]

BORN: December 24, 1745 in County Antrim, Ireland

DIED: September 9, 1806 in Albany, New York

AGE AT DEATH: 60

CAUSE OF DEATH: Unknown

POLITICAL PARTY: Federalist Party

WIVES: Cornelia Bell; Euphemia White

CAREERS: Lawyer, attorney general of New Jersey, United States senator from New Jersey, 2nd governor of New Jersey, associate justice of the Supreme Court of the United States

RELIGION: Presbyterian

NICKNAMES: Mr. Justice (There's no record of Paterson having an actual nickname, but what else would one call a Supreme Court Justice than "Mr. Justice?" Artistic liberty.)

MEMORABLE QUOTE ABOUT HIM: "What may be said of William Paterson as a political leader? Although not an especially original thinker, he was still an able and conscientious representative of his class and party. If on occasion he displayed a fear of unchecked popular government, he, nevertheless, gave full and constant support—and in times of danger—to those ideals on which the American republic is founded: that government emanates from the hands of the people and remains continually responsible to and limited by the constitution as established by the people."[229]

FOUNDING DOCUMENTS SIGNED: The United States Constitution

BOOKS TO READ FOR MORE INFORMATION:

- *William Paterson: His Life and Trials* by Saxe Bannister
- *History of William Paterson and the Darien Company* by James S. Barbour
- *The Lives and Times of the Chief Justices of the United States Supreme Court* by Henry Flanders
- *William Paterson: Lawyer and Statesman, 1745-1806* by John E. O'Connor

11 Things You Never Knew About William Paterson

378. Paterson's family emigrated from Ireland to America in 1747 when William Paterson was 2.
379. William Paterson was a brainiac of sorts: He entered Princeton when he was 14 years old.
380. William Paterson was the judge who presided at the trial of the perpetrators of the Whiskey Rebellion, who had been charged with treason.
381. As a senator, William Paterson helped write the Judiciary Act of 1789.
382. Paterson's Judiciary Act of 1789 established the federal court system still in use today.
383. Paterson helped found the Cliosophic Society at Princeton. And what, you must be wondering, is a Cliosophic Society? It is a debating society. Their topics are literature and politics.
384. George Washington nominated Senator William Paterson for a seat on the United States Supreme Court on February 27, 1793. Washington withdrew the nomination on February 28, 1793, the very next day. Why? Because the president of the United States had violated the Constitution by making the nomination. Washington realized that he had violated Article I, Section 6 of the Constitution, the Ineligibility Clause. The Clause states:

> No Senator or Representative shall, during the Time for which he was elected, be appointed to any civil Office under the Authority of

the United States, which shall have been created, or the Emoluments whereof shall have been increased during such time; and no Person holding any Office under the United States, shall be a Member of either House during his Continuance in Office.

Big "oops!" on the part of POTUS, wouldn't you say? Washington fixed it, though, by waiting until Paterson's senate term had expired and renominating him on March 4, 1793. He was confirmed speedily.

Speaking Words of Wisdom . . .

Have we forgotten this these days?

385. "The education of children is a matter of vast importance and highly deserving of our most serious attention. The prosperity of our country is intimately connected with it; for without morals, there can be no order, and without knowledge, no genuine liberty."[230]

That pretty much sums it up, wouldn't you say?

386. "What is a Constitution? It is the form of government, delineated by the mighty hand of the people, in which certain first principles of fundamental laws are established. . . . it contains the permanent will of the people and is the supreme law of the land."[231]

Property rights rule . . .

387. "It is evident that the right of acquiring and possessing property, and having it protected, is one of the natural, inherent, and unalienable rights of man. Men have a sense of property: Property is necessary to their subsistence, and correspondent to their natural wants and desires; its security was one of the objects, that induced them to unite in society. No man would become a member of a community, in which he could not enjoy the fruits of his honest labour and industry." [232]

Only Congress can declare war . . .

388. "It is the exclusive province of congress to change a state of peace into a state of war."[233]

CHAPTER 26
CHARLES COTESWORTH
PINCKNEY

cc

The legislature of the United States shall pass no law on the subject of religion nor touching or abridging the liberty of the press.[234]

BORN: February 25, 1746 in Charleston, South Carolina

DIED: August 16, 1825 in Charleston, South Carolina

AGE AT DEATH: 79

CAUSE OF DEATH: Unknown

POLITICAL PARTY: Federalist Party

WIFE: Sarah Middleton

CAREERS: Lawyer, planter, soldier, Major General in the Provisional Army, United States minister to France

RELIGION: Episcopalian

MEMORABLE QUOTE ABOUT HIM: "One of the founders of the American Republic. In war he was a companion in arms and friend of Washington. In peace he enjoyed his unchanging confidence."[235]

FOUNDING DOCUMENTS SIGNED: The United States Constitution

BOOKS TO READ FOR MORE INFORMATION:
- *Authentic Copies of the Correspondence of Charles Cotesworth Pinckney, John Marshall, and Elbridge Gerry, Esqrs.* by Charles Cotesworth Pinckney

- *A Founding Family: The Pinckneys of South Carolina* by Frances Leigh Williams
- *Charles Cotesworth Pinckney: Founding Father* by Marvin R. Zahniser

14 Things You Never Knew About Charles Cotesworth Pinckney

389. One of Charles Cotesworth Pinckney's proposals for the new United States was that senators should serve without pay. As you might imagine, that idea did not get very far. (And we cannot help but wonder how the United States would be different today if the only people who served in the Senate did so on a volunteer basis. One potential problem would be only the wealthy would serve. They wouldn't need the paycheck. Would that be a net positive or negative for the country?)

390. Charles Cotesworth Pinckney ran for president as a Federalist twice. Obviously, he lost both times.

391. Charles Cotesworth Pinckney's biographical story is somewhat opposite of those of many of the other Founders and colonists. Pinckney was born in South Carolina in 1745. He was born an American citizen. But in 1753, when he was 8, he was taken to England for his schooling and remained there for 5 years. The family returned to America in 1758, but Pinckney remained behind to study law. This is illustrative of the close ties the colonies had with England prior to 1776. Pinckney's experience was considered ordinary, especially since he came from a wealthy family and everyone knew the best schools were across the pond. As fond as he was of England, when the political pot started over-boiling, he renounced the Crown and embraced the American cause.

392. In 1790, Pinckney was wounded when he was shot in the leg in a duel with Daniel Huger, a South Carolinian planter. Regardless of why they dueled, this event so upset Pinckney that he later began supporting the implementation of laws against dueling. Getting shot can be quite a motivator, apparently.

393. After retiring from politics in 1790, CC devoted himself to education and reading-oriented projects: starting a university, improving the library system, and improving the science of agriculture.

394. Pinckney was a key player in the 1796 XYZ Affair in which France demanded a bribe from him before they'd accept his credentials and discuss shipping issues. He was beyond furious and offended and broke off all

negotiations. During this incident is when it is believed he made his famous proclamation about paying tribute in the form a bribe: "No; no; not a sixpence." (In his eulogy, this quote morphed into, "Millions for defense, not a cent for tribute.") He went home and President John Adams gave him a very high military rank to command troops defend South Carolina.

395. Alexander Hamilton did not like John Adams. This is a true fact. In fact, he once wrote a letter of "critique," let's call it, about Adams. It was 54 pages long. So how far would Hamilton go based on his disdain for the second President? He tried to get Charles Cotesworth Pinckney elected over Adams in the 1800 election. It didn't work.

396. Charles Cotesworth Pinckney learned of his promotion to Major General in the Provisional Army by reading about it in the newspaper on his way home from France in October 1798. He eventually received the official letter. It's hard to conceive of how a government was run and battles were won when communication was by letter.

397. In 1800, one of CCP's soldiers, a man named Captain Davis, committed unspecified "offenses." He wrote to James McHenry and told him that President Adams would not be inattentive to the maxim of Seneca, "let justice be done though the heavens fall." Wonder what he did?

398. On January 9, 1800, CCP wrote to Alexander Hamilton complaining that he was holding 101 French prisoners at Fredrick Town and that the Brigade Inspector did not seem to know that there were supposed to be iron grates on the stockade windows.

Speaking Words of Wisdom . . .

Can't help but wonder how the soldiers responded . . .

399. "If I had a vein that did not beat with the love of my Country, I myself would open it. If I had a drop of blood that could flow dishonourable, I myself would let it out.[236]

The good ole days when we only spent millions for defense . . .

400. "Millions for defense, not a cent for tribute."[237]

CCP hated deserters . . .

401. "There are currently three skulking on the Allegheney Mountain."[238]

402. "I have found many officers in my division very fond of throwing off their uniform and appearing in frocks. I have directed them always to wear their uniforms; we discussed and I think agreed on the propriety of that measure in Philadelphia but I do not see it in the regulations. I wish some general rule was made on the subject."[239]

CHAPTER 27
CHARLES PINCKNEY

So Help Me . . . Wait! What?

Every medium of trade should have an intrinsic value, which paper money has not . . .[240]

BORN: October 26, 1757 in Charles Town, South Carolina

DIED: October 29, 1824 in Charleston, South Carolina

AGE AT DEATH: 67

CAUSE OF DEATH: Unknown, but writings report "failing health" in his last year

POLITICAL PARTY: Federalist Party; also Democratic-Republican

WIFE: Mary Eleanor Laurens

CAREERS: Lawyer, senator for South Carolina, United States minister to Spain, congressman for South Carolina, governor of South Carolina

RELIGION: Episcopalian

NICKNAMES: Constitution Charlie

FOUNDING DOCUMENTS SIGNED: The United States Constitution

BOOKS TO READ FOR MORE INFORMATION:
* *Forgotten Founder: The Life and Times of Charles Pinckney* by Marty D. Mathews
* *A Founding Family: The Pinckneys of South Carolina* by Frances Leigh Williams

9 Things You Never Knew About Charles Pinckney (cousin of CCP from the previous chapter!)

403. Charles Pinckney embraced what most assuredly today be considered vehemently racist views. He defended and practiced slavery, felt Africans were intellectually inferior to whites, and believed that the black race was created by God to serve the white race. At the 1787 Constitutional Convention, Pinckney said, "South Carolina can never receive the plan if it prohibits the slave trade. In every proposed extension of the powers of Congress, South Carolina has expressly and watchfully excepted that of meddling with the importation of negroes."

404. When George Washington toured the southern states in 1791, he stopped at Charles Pinckney's estate, Snee Farm, for breakfast. They ate under an oak tree. In his diary, Washington wrote "breakfasted at the Country seat of Governor Pinckney about 18 miles from our lodging place and then came to the ferry at Haddrells Point."

405. In the 1787 slave inventory of Pinckney's plantation, Snee Farm, it was recorded that he owned 46 slaves valued at approximately $230,000 in today's dollars. Their titles included driver, sawyer, field slave, wheelwright, house wench, carpenter, cooper, gardener, cook, oarsmen, shoemaker, and house servant. There was also listed a woman known as "Old Joan." Next to her name was "Superannuated," which meant "Without value."

406. During the American Revolution, Charles Pinckney was captured by the British and imprisoned.

407. Charles Pinckney was adamantly opposed to giving the president the power to declare and wage war, all that commander in chief stuff notwithstanding. War powers should only be wielded by the Congress. To let the president in on that, he said, "would render the executive a monarchy of the worst kind, to wit, an elective one."

408. As against the government endorsing religion as he was, Charles Pinckney never commented on the ubiquitous presence of "So help me God" in oaths of the time.

Speaking Words of Wisdom . . .

Remember, he said this pre-Bill of Rights

409. "The legislature of the United States shall pass no law on the subject of religion." [241]

"Doodle" Is Not a Compliment

These are the lyrics of the familiar Revolutionary

Charles was a big fan of the gold standard:

410. "I apprehend these general reasonings will be found true with respect to paper money—That experience has shewn, that in every state where it has been practiced since the revolution, it always carries the gold and silver out of the country, and impoverishes it: that while it remains, all the foreign merchants, trading in America, must suffer and lose by it; therefore, that it must ever be a discouragement to commerce: that every medium of trade should have an intrinsic value, which paper money has not; gold and silver are therefore the fittest for this medium, as they are an equivalent, which paper can never be: that debtors in the assemblies will, whenever they can, make paper money with fraudulent views. That in those states where the credit of the paper money has been best supported, the bills have never kept to their nominal value in circulation; but have constantly depreciated to a certain degree."[242]

A French privateer burned a British ship in U.S. waters

411. "[It was] a wanton violation of the neutrality of the United States."[243]

CHAPTER 28
BENJAMIN RUSH

Keepin' It Clean with Dr. Hygiene

Tis done. We have become a nation. [244]

BORN: January 4, 1746 in Byberry, Pennsylvania

DIED: April 19, 1813 in Philadelphia, Pennsylvania

AGE AT DEATH: 67

CAUSE OF DEATH: Typhus fever

POLITICAL PARTY: He supported the policies of the Democratic-Republican Party, and he acted bipartisanly

WIFE: Julia Stockton

CAREERS: Teacher, physician, writer, member of Second Continental Congress, Physician-General of the Constitutional Army

RELIGION: Presbyterian

NICKNAMES: Father of American Psychiatry, Father of American Medicine, Christocrat (he called himself this)

FOUNDING DOCUMENTS SIGNED: Declaration of Independence

BOOKS TO READ FOR MORE INFORMATION:
- *Revolutionary Doctor: Benjamin Rush* (1746–1813) by Carl Binger
- *Benjamin Rush: Patriot and Physician* by Alyn Brodsky
- *Benjamin Rush and His Services to American Education* by Harry G. Good
- *Benjamin Rush: Revolutionary Gadfly* by David Hawke
- *Revolutionary Relationships: Dr. Benjamin Rush* by Matthew Larsen

- *The Selected Writings of Benjamin Rush* by Dagobert D. Runes
- *The Autobiography of Benjamin Rush: His "Travels Through Life" Together with his Commonplace Book for 1789–1813* by Benjamin Rush
- *The Spur of Fame: Dialogues of John Adams and Benjamin Rush, 1805–1813* by Benjamin Rush and John Adams

14 Things You Never Knew About Benjamin Rush

412. Benjamin Rush was the only signer of the Declaration of Independence who had a medical degree.
413. In 1786, Benjamin Rush opened a free hospital for the poor and indigent in Philadelphia. This hospital was the first of its kind in America.
414. Benjamin Rush believed that bleeding and purging could cure yellow fever. It can't, and those on the receiving end of his "treatment" often ended up in worse condition than before they sought help.
415. Benjamin Rush's medical beliefs and practices evolved as he aged and studied more. He was one of the first medical practitioners to conclude that mental illness was not due to demonic possession. He was also on the cutting edge of putting into practical use hygienic practices to prevent illness; i.e., acceptance of the germ theory.
416. Two of the notables who delivered eulogies at Rush's funeral were Thomas Jefferson and John Adams.
417. Benjamin Rush was against capital punishment, a remarkably progressive position considering the times.
418. Benjamin Rush was very upset about the late-in-life animosity between Thomas Jefferson and John Adams. In October 1809, Rush had a dream in which Jefferson and Adams were reconciled and were participating in a great exchange of letters. Rush wrote to both men and told them of his dream. This facilitated a rekindling of the former Presidents' friendship and the ultimate result was, indeed, a great exchange of letters between Jefferson and Adams, until their deaths within three hours of each other on July 4, 1826.
419. Benjamin Rush was a religious fellow. In fact, he stated on more than once occasion that he supported all youth being educated in the Christian way. Guess he felt that an exception to that ol' First Amendment was justified when it came to schooling youngsters.

Speaking Words of Wisdom . . .

Stupid is as stupid does . . .

420. "Freedom can exist only in the society of knowledge. Without learning, men are incapable of knowing their rights."[245]

Europe sucks . . .

421. "Europe resembles an old garment that has been turned. The habits of your people forbid every species of improvement in human happiness. In America, everything is new and yielding. Here, genius and benevolence may have full scope. Here the benefactor of mankind may realize all his schemes."[246]

Segars?

422. "Who can see groups of boys of 6 or 8 years old in our streets smoking segars, without anticipating such a depreciation of our posterity in health and character, as can scarcely be contemplated at this distance of time without pain and horror."[247]

And back then, capital punishment was not "gentle" . . .

423. "Every man possesses an absolute power over his own liberty and property, but not over his own life. The punishment of murder by death, is contrary to reason, and to the order and happiness of society. The punishment of murder by death, is contrary to divine revelation."[248.]

Rush: Not a big fan of the clergy . . .

424. "I agree with you likewise in your wishes to keep religion and government independant [sic] of each Other. Were it possible for St. Paul to rise from his grave at the present juncture, he would say to the Clergy who are now so active in settling the political Affairs of the World, 'Cease from your political labors your kingdom is not of this World. Read my Epistles. In no part of them will you perceive me aiming to depose a pagan Emperor, or to place a Christian upon a throne.' Christianity disdains to receive Support from human Governments. From this, it derives its preeminence over all the religions that ever have, or ever

Shall exist in the World. Human Governments may receive Support from Christianity but it must be only from the love of justice, and peace which it is calculated to produce in the minds of men. By promoting these, and all the Other Christian Virtues by your precepts, and example, you will much sooner overthrow errors of all kind, and establish our pure and holy religion in the World, than by aiming to produce by your preaching, or pamphlets [sic] any change in the political state of mankind."[249]

Teach the Bible in public schools? Didn't we already deal with this in 1776?

425. "But passing by all other considerations, and contemplating merely the political institutions of the United States, I lament that we waste so much time and money in punishing crimes and take so little pains to prevent them. We profess to be republicans, and yet we neglect the only means of establishing and perpetuating our republican forms of government; that is, the universal education of our youth in the principles of Christianity by means of the Bible; for this divine book, above all others, favors that equality among mankind, that respect for just laws, and all those sober and frugal virtues which constitute the soul of republicanism."[250]

A FEW NASTY THINGS JOHN ADAMS SAID ABOUT OTHER FOUNDERS

Bob Dole called John Adams an "18th century Don Rickles." Here is proof of the validity of that statement.

- On **George Washington**: "That Washington is not a scholar is certain. That he is too illiterate, unlearned, unread for his station is equally beyond dispute."
- On **Thomas Jefferson**: "His soul is poisoned with ambition." Also, he is "a mean-spirited, low-lived fellow, the son of a half-breed Indian squaw, sired by a Virginia mulatto father."
- On **Benjamin Franklin**: "His whole life has been one continued insult to good manners and to decency."
- On **Alexander Hamilton**: "That bastard brat of a Scottish peddler! His ambition, his restlessness, and all his grandiose schemes come, I'm convinced, from a superabundance of secretions, which he couldn't find enough whores to absorb!"
- On **Thomas Paine's** *Common Sense*: "What a poor, ignorant, malicious, short sighted, crapulous mass."

CHAPTER 29
ROGER SHERMAN

The Shoemaker Senator

The question is, not what rights naturally belong to man, but how they may be most equally and effectually guarded in society.

BORN: April 19, 1721 in Newton, Massachusetts

DIED: July 23, 1793 in New Haven, Connecticut

AGE AT DEATH: 72

CAUSE OF DEATH: Typhoid fever

POLITICAL PARTY: Pro-Administration

WIVES: Rebecca Minot Prescott; Elizabeth Hartwell

CAREERS: Shoemaker; surveyor; lawyer; Justice of the Peace; 1st mayor of New Haven, Connecticut; Connecticut delegate to the First Continental Congress, Connecticut Congressman in the House of Representatives; United States senator from Connecticut

RELIGION: Congregationalist

NICKNAMES: The Old Puritan

MEMORABLE QUOTES ABOUT HIM: "That is Mr. Sherman, of Connecticut, a man who never said a foolish thing in his life."[251]

"He deserves infinite praise, no man has a better heart nor a clearer head. If he cannot embellish he can furnish thoughts that are wise and useful. He is an able politician, and extremely artful in accomplishing any particular object; it is remarked that he seldom fails."[252]

"He is as cunning as the Devil, and if you attack him, you ought to know him well; he is not easily managed, but if he suspects you are trying to take him in, you may as well catch an Eel by the tail."[253]

"[He was] as honest as an angel and as firm in the cause of American Independence as Mount Atlas."[254]

FOUNDING DOCUMENTS SIGNED: The Declaration of Independence, the Articles of Confederation, the United States Constitution

BOOKS TO READ FOR MORE INFORMATION:
- *Roger Sherman, Signer and Statesman* by Roger Sherman Boardman
- *The Life of Roger Sherman* by Lewis Henry Boutell
- *Roger Sherman's Connecticut: Yankee Politics and the American Revolution* by Christopher Collier
- *Roger Sherman and the Creation of the American Republic* by Mark David Hall

19 Things You Never Knew About Roger Sherman

426. Roger Sherman never went to law school, but was admitted to the Connecticut Bar in 1754.
427. Roger Sherman was fruitful. He had 15 children with 2 wives: 7 with Elizabeth Hartwell Sherman, and 8 with Rebecca Minot Prescott Sherman.
428. Sherman believed that in order to maintain fiscal health, states should impose high taxes rather than borrow money or issue currency.
429. Sherman was greatly respected by Thomas Jefferson, who once said, "That is Mr. Sherman, of Connecticut, a man who never said a foolish thing in his life."[255]
430. One of Sherman's descendants was Archibald Cox, the Special Prosecutor during President Nixon's Watergate scandal.
431. John Adams described Sherman as "one of the most sensible men in the world. The clearest head and the steadiest heart. Mr. Sherman was one of the soundest and strongest pillars of the revolution."[256]
432. Sherman was one of only two Founding Fathers who signed the three bulwark documents of our republic—the Declaration of Independence, the Articles of Confederation, and the Constitution.
433. Roger Sherman was the treasurer of Yale University for many years. Sherman's involvement with Yale started out by, as the proprietor of the first general store in New Haven, selling goods to Yale students.
434. Roger Sherman was responsible for the construction of the Yale campus chapel.

435. One of the enduring legends about Roger Sherman is that when he decided to move to New Milford, Connecticut (where his brother lived) from Stoughton, Massachusetts in 1743, he walked the entire distance—around 125 miles—with his cobbler's tools on his back. At an average human walking speed of 3 miles per hour, it probably took him around 42 hours to get there. If he walked for 10 hours a day, he was there in 4-5 days.

436. Roger Sherman believed the federal government had 4, and only 4 sovereign duties:
   "First, defense against foreign danger; secondly, against internal disputes and a resort to force; thirdly, treaties with foreign nations; fourthly, regulating foreign commerce, and drawing revenue from it."

437. He said, "All other matters, civil and criminal, would be much better left in the hands of the states."

Speaking Words of Wisdom . . .

Freedom is . . .

438. "If you suffer any man to govern you who is not strongly interested in supporting your privileges, you will certainly lose them."[257]

439. "Every free-man shou'd promote the public good."[258]

We're in charge, King G., not you . . .

440. "The Parliament of Great Britain had authority to make laws for America in no case whatever."[259]

And we added an Amendment to be sure . . .

441. "Congress has no power to make any religious establishments." [260]

Seems Sherman was definitely a Christian, wouldn't you agree?

442. "I believe that there is one only living and true God, existing in three persons, the Father, the Son, and the Holy Ghost."

Wise words . . .

443. "When you are in the minority, talk; when you are in the majority, vote."

The hidden motive for flattering the president . . .

444. "If the president alone was vested with the power of appointing all officers, and was left to select a council for himself, he would be liable to be deceived by flatterers and pretenders to patriotism."[261]

JOHN HANSON, 1ST PRESIDENT OF THE UNITED STATES . . . WAIT . . . WHAT?

The Articles of Confederation served as America's first Constitution.

As mentioned in the chapter "What Are America's Founding Documents," the Articles of Confederation didn't really work that well. They did create a federal government, but it didn't have an executive branch and only allowed for a kind of ceremonial president, what they called "President of the United States in Congress Assembled."

John Hanson was the very first "President of the United States in Congress Assembled." He hated the job, which came with a 1-year term, and which was boring and consisted of signing documents and responding to correspondence.

The reason John Hanson was not the first president of the United States is because he did not serve under the United States Constitution, which hadn't been written yet. Some people like to fool around with this piece of arcane historical trivia by asking people, "Did you know that George Washington was not the first president of the United States? John Hanson was."

He wasn't. He was a member of the Continental Congress from 1780–1782, and while in office he approved the Great Seal of the United States, but first United States president? No.

CHAPTER 30
JAMES WILSON

The Detailer

The happiness of the society is the first law of every government.[262]

BORN: September 14, 1742 in Carskerdo, Great Britain

DIED: August 21, 1798 in Edentown, North Carolina

AGE AT DEATH: 55

CAUSE OF DEATH: Stroke after a bout of malaria

POLITICAL PARTY: Federalist Party

WIVES: Rachel Bird; Hannah Gray

CAREERS: Associate justice of the Supreme Court of the United States, professor of law at the College of Philadelphia

RELIGION: Episcopalian, Presbyterian

NICKNAMES:

MEMORABLE QUOTE ABOUT HIM: "Tracing over the events of Wilson's life, we are impressed by the lucid quality of his mind. With this went a restless energy and insatiable ambition, an almost frightening vitality that turned with undiminished energy and enthusiasm to new tasks and new ventures. Yet, when all has been said, the inner man remains, despite our probings, an enigma."[263]

FOUNDING DOCUMENTS SIGNED: The Declaration of Independence, the United States Constitution

14 Things You Never Knew About James Wilson

445. Not many people liked James Wilson. And that was truly ironic. Wilson came off as a snooty, wealthy "1-percenter" who couldn't relate to the common folk. Yet, he spent much of his career fighting for the rights of the common folk. Perception sometimes isn't everything.

446. James Wilson was a legal scholar who was passed over for the Supreme Court 3 times.

447. In his waning years, Wilson was broke. And since there was no Consumer Financial Protection Bureau in those days, Wilson was hounded, as he put it, "like a wild beast" by creditors.

448. James Wilson's first job in America after emigrating from Scotland was as a Latin tutor at the College of Philadelphia.

449. James Wilson is credited with coming up with the concept of "consent of the governed." He discussed in an essay he wrote in 1768 titled *Considerations on the Nature and Extent of the Legislative Authority of the British Parliament.*

450. In 1774, 6 years after his important "Considerations" essay, he wrote, "all men are, by nature, equal and free: no one has a right to any authority over another without his consent: all lawful government is founded on the consent of those who are subject to it."

451. James Wilson was the first professor of law at the College of Philadelphia. He was given the title and post in 1790.

452. Can a citizen of one state sue the government of another state? James Wilson ruled yes; the Eleventh Amendment was thus drafted and ratified to overturn his decision. The Eleventh Amendment reads, "The judicial power of the United States shall not be construed to extend to any suit in law or equity, commenced or prosecuted against one of the United States by citizens of another state, or by citizens or subjects of any foreign state." This established sovereign immunity.

Speaking Words of Wisdom . . .

Only the Pope can get away with claiming infallibility . . .

453. "When I deliver my sentiments from this chair, they shall be my honest sentiments: when I deliver them from the bench, they shall be nothing more. In both places I shall make, because I mean to support, the claim to integrity: in neither shall I make, because, in neither, can I support, the claim to infallibility."[264]

Childrearing 101 . . .

454. "It is the duty of parents to maintain their children decently, and according to their circumstances; to protect them according to the dictates of prudence; and to educate them according to the suggestions of a judicious and zealous regard for their usefulness, their respectability and happiness."[265]

Don't do the crime if you can't do the time . . .

455. "To prevent crimes, is the noblest end and aim of criminal jurisprudence. To punish them, is one of the means necessary for the accomplishment of this noble end and aim."[266]

Wilson defined when life began . . .

456. "With consistency, beautiful and undeviating, human life, from its commencement to its close, is protected by the common law. In the contemplation of law, life begins when the infant is first able to stir in the womb. By the law, life is protected not only from immediate destruction, but from every degree of actual violence, and, in some cases, from every degree of danger."[267]

Slavery is "unauthorized . . ."

457. "Slavery, or an absolute and unlimited power in the master over the life and fortune of the slave, is unauthorized by the common law . . . The reasons which we sometimes see assigned for the origin and the continuance of slavery appear, when examined to the bottom, to be built upon a false foundation. In the enjoyment of their persons and of their property, the common law protects all."[268]

458. "This system will not hurry us into war; it is calculated to guard against it. It will not be in the power of a single man, or a single body of men, to involve us in such distress; for the important power of declaring war is vested in the legislature at large."[269]

CHAPTER 31
JOHN WITHERSPOON

Mr. Princeton

There are times when the mind may be expected to be more awake to divine truth, and the conscience more open to the arrows of conviction than at others. A season of public judgment is of this kind.[270]

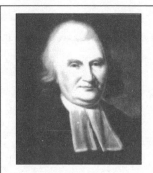

BORN: February 5, 1723 in Gifford, East Lothian, Scotland

DIED: November 15, 1794 in Princeton, New Jersey

AGE AT DEATH: 71

CAUSE OF DEATH: Unknown. Eye injuries blinded him two years prior to his death.

WIVES: Elizabeth Montgomery, Ann Marshall

CAREERS: President of Princeton University, member of the Second Continental Congress, clergyman and theologian

RELIGION: Presbyterian

NICKNAMES: Our Old Scotch Sachem (coined by Benjamin Rush), Scotch Granite, John Knox Redivivus

MEMORABLE QUOTE ABOUT HIM: "One quality remarkable, and highly deserving imitation in him was, his attention to young persons. He never suffered an opportunity to escape him of imparting the most useful advice to them, according to their circumstances, when they happened to be in his company. And this was always done in so agreeable a way, that they could neither be inattentive to it, nor was it possible to forget it. On his domestic virtues I shall only say, he was an affectionate husband, a tender parent, and a kind master ; to which I may add, he was a sincere and a warm friend.— But, I hasten to consider him as a scholar, and a director of the system of education in the college."[271]

FOUNDING DOCUMENTS SIGNED: The Articles of Confederation, the Declaration of Independence

BOOKS TO READ FOR MORE INFORMATION:

- *President Witherspoon: A Biography*, 2 vols. Varnum L. Collins
- *John Witherspoon and the Founding of the American Republic* by Jeffrey H. Morrison
- *The Selected Writings of John Witherspoon* by Thomas P. Miller
- *John Witherspoon: An American Leader* by Matthew F. Rose
- *John Witherspoon: Parson, Politician, Patriot* by Martha Lou Lemmon Stohlman

14 Things You Never Knew About John Witherspoon

459. John Witherspoon could read the Bible at the age of 4.
460. John Witherspoon is responsible for us calling the buildings and grounds of a college or university a "campus." He used it in 1768 to describe the setting of Princeton University (then known as the College of New Jersey), and the term stuck.
461. As a professor at Princeton, John Witherspoon ultimately ended up teaching a United States president and vice president, 9 cabinet officers, 21 senators, 39 congressmen, 3 justices of the Supreme Court, and 12 state governors.
462. In 1736, John Witherspoon entered the University of Edinburgh at the age of 13. Smart boy.
463. One of John Witherspoon's first published works was *Ecclesiastical characteristics: or, the arcana of church policy. . . . wherein is shewn a plain and easy way of attaining to the character of a moderate . . . in the Church of Scotland*, which he originally released anonymously at the age of thirty. This work was a satire of a certain clergyman and became incredibly popular. Certain Scottish clergy, however, were infuriated and Witherspoon had to defend the work before a church synod.

The opening passage of *Ecclesiastical Characteristics* suggests why they were pissed:

All ecclesiastical persons, of whatever rank, whether principals of colleges, professors of divinity, ministers, or even probationers, that are suspected of heresy, are to be esteemed men of great genius, vast learning, and uncommon worth; and are, by all means, to be supported and protected.[272]

An excerpt from Witherspoon's defense:

"The *Ecclesiastical Characteristics* is evidently a satire upon clergymen of a certain character. It is a satire too, which every body must see was intended to carry in it no small measure of keenness and severity. This was to be expected from the nature and design of the performance. A satire that does not bite is good for nothing. Hence it necessarily follows, that it is essential to this manner of writing to provoke and give offence. . . ."[273]

One cannot help but admire a man who would state with forthright certainty, "It is essential to . . . give offence."

464. Witherspoon's elevation to president of Princeton was delayed for years because his wife was too afraid to cross the Atlantic in a ship. She finally marshaled the courage and they made the trip together in 1768.

465. John Witherspoon was the only clergyman to sign the Declaration of Independence.

466. In November 1776, Witherspoon evacuated Princeton because the British were coming. Come they did, and they wrecked the place.

467. When John Witherspoon married his 2nd wife, Ann Marshall, she was 24 and he was 68.

Speaking Words of Wisdom . . .

Good tip

468. "Never rise to speak till you have something to say; and when you have said it, cease."

Mixing politics with religion . . . a dangerous combination

469. "You are all my witnesses, that this is the first time of my introducing any political subject into the pulpit. At this season, however, it is not only lawful but necessary, and I willingly embrace the opportunity of declaring my opinion without any hesitation, that the cause in which America is now in arms, is the cause of justice, of liberty, and of human nature."[274]

Sadly, this is oft necessary

470. "Never read a book through merely because you have begun it."

A preacher against decadence? What a surprise, eh?

471. "Nothing is more certain than that a general profligacy and corruption of manners make a people ripe for destruction. A good form of government may hold the rotten materials together for some time, but beyond a certain pitch, even the best constitution will be ineffectual, and slavery must ensue." [275]

A noble idea . . .

472. "I beseech you to make a wise improvement of the present threatening aspect of public affairs and to remember that your duty to God, to your country, to your families, and to yourselves, is the same."[276]

---

5 WAYS THE COLONISTS INSULTED KING GEORGE

1. They sang insulting songs about him.
2. The publicly trashed him as a drunkard and tyrant.
3. They refused to pay his taxes and smuggled taxed goods into the colonies.
4. They burned him in effigy.
5. They hung him in effigy.

CHAPTER 32
GEORGE WYTHE

Pronounced "With" Not "Wythe"

I am murdered.

BORN: 1726 in Elizabeth City County, Virginia

DIED: June 8, 1806 in Richmond, Virginia

AGE AT DEATH: 80

CAUSE OF DEATH: Murder. He was poisoned by his nephew.

POLITICAL PARTY: Federalist Party/Anti-Federalist Party

WIVES: Ann Lewis; Elizabeth Taliaferro

CAREERS: Lawyer; planter, teacher, philanthropist, chancellor of Virginia; judge; professor of law and police; delegate to the Second Continental Congress; member of Virginia House of Burgess; mayor of Williamsburg, Virginia; attorney general, Virginia

RELIGION: Episcopalian

NICKNAMES: The Father of American Jurisprudence, America's First Law Professor, the American Aristides

MEMORABLE QUOTE ABOUT HIM: "He was my ancient master, my earliest and best friend, and to him I am indebted for first impressions which have [been] the most salutary on the course of my life."[277]

"Superior to popular prejudices, and every corrupting influence, nothing could induce him to swerve from truth and right. In his decisions, he seemed to be a pure intelligence, untouched by human passions, and settling the disputes of men, according to the dictates of eternal and immutable justice."[278]

FOUNDING DOCUMENT SIGNED: Declaration of Independence

BOOKS TO READ FOR MORE INFORMATION:
- *Jefferson's Second Father* by John Bailey
- *George Wythe of Williamsburg* by Joyce Blackburn
- *I Am Murdered: George Wythe, Thomas Jefferson, and the Killing That Shocked a New Nation* by Bruce Chadwick

15 Things You Never Knew About George Wythe

473. George Wythe (pronounced "with") was probably murdered by arsenic poisoning by his grandnephew and heir George Wythe Sweeney. Wythe suspected Sweeney of the poisoning and was able to disinherit him before he died. Wythe also freed his slaves in his will.

474. George Wythe's maid claimed she saw Wythe's grandnephew Sweeney throw something (probably the arsenic) in the fire the morning Wythe was poisoned, but her eyewitness testimony could not be used during Sweeney's trial. No African-American was allowed to testify against a white person in court.

475. George Wythe was the first law professor to make American constitutional law a course of study.

476. George Wythe carried out his own "ice bucket challenge" every morning upon awakening. He would head out to his well, fill a bucket with ice cold water, and pour it over himself.

477. George Wythe's usual breakfast consisted of eggs, toast, sweetbread, and coffee.

478. After Wythe lost both his parents at a young age, he apparently turned into a party guy. A party guy with money. Although he was under the guardianship of his older brother Thomas, he still surrendered to . . . well, you can figure out for yourself what he surrendered to after reading this description of this period in young George Wythe's life from an 1856 biography of the signers of the Declaration of Independence:

Being deprived, at this unguarded period of life, of the counsel and example of these natural guardians, he became devoted, for several years, to amusement and dissipation, to which he was strongly enticed by the fortune that had been left him. During this period, his literary pursuits were almost entirely neglected; and there was the greatest reason to fear he would not escape that vortex into which so many young men remedilessly sink. [279]

479. George Wythe's wife Elizabeth Taliaferro, who Wythe married in 1754 at the age of 15, was of Italian descent. Her distant ancestor Bartholomew Taliaferro was born in Italy in 1532. Elizabeth died in 1787 at the age of 48. Their only child died in infancy.
480. One of George Wythe's students was Thomas Jefferson.
481. George Wythe designed the official Seal of Virginia.
482. George Wythe was a tough teacher. He would routinely make a student come to his home before the student had breakfast. He would then have the student translate Greek into English without using a Greek dictionary, and only then could the boy leave to go home and have breakfast.
483. George Wythe left Thomas Jefferson books and manuscripts in his will, but he also left him "my silver cups and gold headed cane."[280]

Speaking Words of Wisdom . . .

484. "I give my books and small philosophical apparatus to Thomas Jefferson, President of the United States of America: a legacy considered abstract lie, perhaps not deserving a place in his museum, but, estimated by my good will to him, the most valuable to him of any thing which I have the power to bestow."[281]

George had a motto . . .

485. "Upright in prosperity and perils."[282]

George had a motive . . .

486. "[My purpose is] to "form such characters as may be fit to succeed those which have been ornamental and useful in the national councils of America."[283]

He'd point at the Constitution . . .

487. "If the whole legislature, an event to be deprecated, should attempt to overlap the bounds, prescribed to them by the people, I, in administering

the public justice of the country, will meet the united powers at my seat in this tribunal; and, pointing to the Constitution, will say to them, here is the limit of your authority; and hither shall you go, but no further."[284]

IT'S ALL RELATIVE

12 Surprising Family Connections of the Founding Fathers

Someone's apparently done the math, and it seems that everyone on earth is everyone else's 50th cousin. And this has been true for centuries. This is how Barack Obama and Paris Hilton are related to George Washington, and how Muhammad Ali and Ray Bradbury are related to James Madison.

This feature is a look at some famous relatives of some famous founders.

488. The following people are related to GEORGE WASHINGTON:

General George S. Patton, Queen Elizabeth II, Steve McQueen, Jane Seymour, Jonathan Swift, Ralph Waldo Emerson, Franklin Delano Roosevelt, Princess Diana, John Kerry, Humphrey Bogart, Tennessee Williams, Lee Harvey Oswald, Herbert Hoover, Christopher Reeve, Ted Danson, Paris Hilton, Ellen DeGeneres. Grover Cleveland, L. Frank Baum, Marilyn Monroe, Grace Slick, Amelia Earhart, Mitt Romney, John Hinckley Jr., Julia Child, Thomas Pynchon, George W. Bush, Richard Gere, Britney Spears, Charles Darwin, Bing Crosby, Roy Rogers, Alexander Hamilton, Robert Frost, Orson Welles, Barack Obama, Brad Pitt, Walt Disney, Matt Damon, Eli Whitney, Vincent Price, Valerie Bertinelli, Herman Melville, Truman Capote, Dick Cheney, Ernest Hemingway, Judy Garland, the Wright Brothers, Nathaniel Hawthorne.

489. The following people are related to THOMAS JEFFERSON:

Jennifer Lawrence, Harper Lee, Upton Sinclair, Susan B. Anthony, Charles Darwin, Jane Seymour, Winston Churchill, John McCain, James Madison, Meriwether Lewis, Zachary Taylor, Francis Scott Key, John Kerry, Olivia De Haviland, Humphrey Bogart, Dick Clark, Jimmy Carter, Norman Rockwell, Alan Shepard, Elizabeth Montgomery, Kyra Sedgwick, Hugh Grant, Kate Upton, Carly Fiorina, Noël Coward, Theodore Roosevelt, Sally Ride, Ray Bradbury, Lizzie Borden, Katharine Hepburn, Eli Whitney, Anderson Cooper, Sarah Palin.

490. The following people are related to BENJAMIN FRANKLIN:

J. A. Folger, Amy Poehler.

491. The following people are related to ALEXANDER HAMILTON:

Jane Seymour, Johnny Mercer, Robert Louis Stevenson, Howard Dean, Princess Diana, Helen Keller, Noël Coward, Eleanor Roosevelt, Jonathan Swift, Charles Darwin, John D. Rockefeller, Hugh Grant, Eli Whitney, Francis Scott Key, Emily

Post, Admiral Richard Byrd, Tennessee Williams, Humphrey Bogart, Orson Welles, Harper Lee, Norman Rockwell, Sandra Day O'Connor, Joanne Woodward, Keri Russell, Ellen DeGeneres, Gloria Vanderbilt, General Douglas MacArthur, Barbara Bush, Lizzie Borden, Bing Crosby, Pete Seeger, Roy Rogers, Oliver Platt, Gerald Ford, Chevy Chase, Ralph Waldo Emerson, Jack London, Lee Harvey Oswald, Bette Davis, Jesse James, Matt Damon, Harriet Beecher Stowe, Samuel Colt, Rutherford B. Hayes.

492. **The following people are related to** James Madison:

Zachary Taylor, General George S. Patton, Meriwether Lewis, Joanne Woodward, Barack Obama, Brad Pitt, Lee Harvey Oswald, William Henry Harrison, Muhammad Ali, Robert Frost, Jack London, Joan Fontaine, Bing Crosby, Calvin Coolidge, Alan Shepard, Alan Ladd, Christopher Reeve, Jane Fonda, Ted Danson, Eli Whitney, Marilyn Monroe, Mitt Romney, Ray Bradbury, Linda Hamilton, Grover Cleveland, John Hancock, Pete Seeger, Bette Davis, Ernest Hemingway, Truman Capote.

493. **The following people are related to** James Madison:

Zachary Taylor, General George S. Patton, Meriwether Lewis, Adlai Stevenson II, Edith Wilson, Joanne Woodward, Barack Obama, Brad Pitt, General Robert E. Lee, Helen Keller, Steve McQueen, Theodore Roosevelt, Eleanor Roosevelt, Lee Harvey Oswald, William Henry Harrison, Muhammad Ali, Anne Boleyn, Prince William, Jane Seymour, Robert Frost, Jack London, John Kerry, Princess Diana, Norman Rockwell, George Washington, Thomas Jefferson, Franklin D. Roosevelt, Charles Darwin, Susan B. Anthony, Frank Lloyd Wright, Bill Nye, Jane Fonda, Paris Hilton, Richard Nixon, Ray Bradbury, Jesse James, Sarah Palin, Linda Hamilton, Sydney Biddle Barrows, Abigail Adams, Bette Davis, Liz Claiborne, Ernest Hemingway.

494. **The following people are related to** John Adams:

Raquel Welch, Abigail Adams, Henry Wadsworth Longfellow, Edgar Rice Burroughs, Emily Dickinson, Calvin Coolidge, Tennessee Williams, Emily Post, Thomas Pynchon, Marilyn Monroe, John Steinbeck, Orson Welles, Julia Child, Dick Van Dyke, James Brolin, Jodie Foster, Kim Kardashian, Ralph Waldo Emerson, Louisa May Alcott, Millard Fillmore, Burgess Meredith, Lee Remick, Ellen DeGeneres.

495. **The following people are related to** Patrick Henry:

Anne Boleyn, Jane Seymour, Alexander Hamilton, Johnny Mercer, Princess Diana, Howard Dean, General Robert E. Lee, Helen Keller, Noël Coward, Theodore Roosevelt, Charles Darwin, Winston Churchill, Hugh Grant, Zachary Taylor, Jonathan Swift, Francis Scott Key, Emily Post, Orson Welles, Robert Louis Stevenson, Dick Clark, Ted Danson, Sally Ride, John Foster Dulles, Mamie Eisenhower, Marilyn Monroe, John Hancock, Aaron Burr, Nathaniel Hawthorne.

496. The following people are related to SAMUEL ADAMS:

Raquel Welch, Ralph Waldo Emerson, Edgar Rice Burroughs, Emily Dickinson, John Steinbeck, Anthony Perkins, James Spader, Halle Berry, Richard Nixon, James Dean, Humphrey Bogart, Ray Bradbury, Lucille Ball, Thomas Pynchon, John Lithgow, Bette Davis.

497. The following people are related to JOHN HANCOCK:

Ralph Waldo Emerson, Alan Shepard, Pete Seeger, James Spader, Matt Damon, the Wright Brothers, Norman Rockwell, Dick Clark, Abraham Lincoln, Herman Melville, Robert Frost, Gerald Ford, Sally Field, Bette Davis, Grover Cleveland, Anne Boleyn, Elizabeth Montgomery, Princess Diana, Bing Crosby, Jane Fonda, Kate Upton, Noël Coward, Charles Darwin, William Howard Taft, Ernest Hemingway, Judy Garland, Frank Lloyd Wright, Susan B. Anthony, Jack London, Walt Disney, Eli Whitney, Nathaniel Hawthorne.

498. The following people are related to ROGER SHERMAN:

George H. W. Bush, George W. Bush, Eli Whitney, Jeb Bush, Sarah Palin, Franklin D. Roosevelt, General Douglas MacArthur, Susan B. Anthony, Calvin Coolidge, William Howard Taft, Winston Churchill, Christopher Lloyd, Herbert Hoover, Janis Joplin, Marilyn Monroe, Harriet Beecher Stowe, Tennessee Williams, Henry Fonda, Norman Rockwell, John Steinbeck, Princess Diana, Valerie Bertinelli, Humphrey Bogart, Bing Crosby, Vincent Price, John Quincy Adams, Grover Cleveland, Harper Lee, Lizzie Borden, Richard Gere, Noël Coward, Hugh Grant, Chevy Chase, Upton Sinclair, Jack London, Walt Disney, George Hamilton, Jesse James, Vachel Lindsay.

499. The following people are related to GEORGE MASON:

Paris Hilton, Jane Seymour, Anne Boleyn, General Robert E. Lee, Princess Diana, Stephen Crane, Dick Clark, Herbert Hoover, L. Frank Baum, Edgar Rice Burroughs, Fannie Farmer, Grace Slick, John Hinckley Jr., Julia Child, Thomas Pynchon, Alec Baldwin, Paget Brewster, Elisabeth Shue, Ileana Douglas, Britney Spears, Marshall Field, Dick Cheney, Aaron Burr.

Special thanks to the website **www.FamousKin.com** from which many of these names were drawn. Unlike this simple listing of names, however, the fine folks at Famous Kin actually did the research to determine precisely how Sarah Palin was related to Thomas Jefferson. (She's his 16th cousin 5 times removed via Blanche of Artois.) This website is highly recommended for genealogical research on historical figures.

59 Founders Who Signed The Declaration of Independence, The United States Constitution, Or Both

Josiah Bartlett • Richard Bassett • Gunning Bedford Jr. • John Blair Jr.
• Carter Braxton • David Brearley • Jacob Broom • Pierce Butler
• Daniel Carroll • Samuel Chase • Abraham Clark • George Clymer
• Jonathan Dayton • William Ellery • William Few • Thomas Fitzsimons
• William Floyd • Nicholas Gilman • Nathaniel Gorham • Button Gwinnett
• Lyman Hall • Cornelius Harnett • Benjamin Harrison V • John Hart
• Joseph Hewes • Thomas Heyward Jr. • William Hooper • Stephen Hopkins
• Samuel Huntington • Jared Ingersoll • William Samuel Johnson
• John Langdon • Francis Lightfoot Lee • Francis Lewis • Philip Livingston
• William Livingston • Thomas Lynch Jr. • James McHenry • Thomas McKean
• Arthur Middleton • Lewis Morris • Thomas Nelson Jr. • William Paca
• Robert Treat Paine • John Penn • George Reed • Caesar Rodney
• George Ross • John Rutledge • James Smith • Richard Dobbs Spaight
• Richard Stockton • Thomas Stone • George Taylor • Matthew Thornton
• George Walton • William Whipple • William Williams
• Hugh Williamson • Oliver Wolcott

More Founders Who Signed the Declaration of Independence, the United States Constitution, or Both

This book takes a look at 32 indispensable and invaluable Founding Fathers, men many would call the most memorable of the FF crew.

We chose to write about Founding Fathers who had interesting life stories, who made a major contribution to the writing of our Founding Documents, or who made major decisions that greatly impacted the country's origin.

But there were many, many more people involved in the conception, development, and establishment of the United States of America. The following 59 men, all of whom made a contribution to the birth of America and who are considered Founding Fathers, all signed either the Declaration of Independence, the United States Constitution, or both.

JOSIAH BARTLETT

Born: November 21, 1729 in Amesbury, Massachusetts

Died: May 19, 1795 in Kingston, New Hampshire

Age at Death: 65

Founding Document Signed: The Declaration of Independence

Dɪᴅ Yᴏᴜ Kɴᴏw? Josiah Bartlett is the ancestor of the fictional President Josiah Bartlet on the extremely popular TV show *The West Wing*.

RICHARD BASSETT

Bᴏʀɴ: April 2, 1745 in Cecil County, Maryland, British America

Dɪᴇᴅ: September 15, 1815 in Kent County, Delaware

Aɢᴇ ᴀᴛ Dᴇᴀᴛʜ: 70

Fᴏᴜɴᴅɪɴɢ Dᴏᴄᴜᴍᴇɴᴛ Sɪɢɴᴇᴅ: The United States Constitution

Dɪᴅ Yᴏᴜ Kɴᴏw? Richard Bassett was a big supporter of moving the United States capitol from New York City to Washington, D. C. And guess what? It happened.

GUNNING BEDFORD JR.

Bᴏʀɴ: April 13, 1747 in Philadelphia, Pennsylvania

Dɪᴇᴅ: March 30, 1812 in Wilmington, Delaware

Aɢᴇ ᴀᴛ Dᴇᴀᴛʜ: 64

Fᴏᴜɴᴅɪɴɢ Dᴏᴄᴜᴍᴇɴᴛ ѕɪɢɴᴇᴅ: The United States Constitution

Dɪᴅ Yᴏᴜ Kɴᴏw? William Pierce described Gunning Bedford Jr., as "tempestuous" and "corpulent."

JOHN BLAIR JR.

Bᴏʀɴ: April 17, 1732 in Williamsburg, Virginia

Dɪᴇᴅ: September 12, 1800 in Williamsburg, Virginia, U.S.

Aɢᴇ ᴀᴛ Dᴇᴀᴛʜ: 68

Fᴏᴜɴᴅɪɴɢ Dᴏᴄᴜᴍᴇɴᴛ Sɪɢɴᴇᴅ: The United States Constitution

Dɪᴅ Yᴏᴜ Kɴᴏw? Because Justice John Blair Jr. couldn't find an answer in the Constitution as to whether or not a citizen could sue a state, the Eleventh Amendment was drafted and ratified.

CARTER BRAXTON

Bᴏʀɴ: September 16, 1736 in King and Queen County, Virginia

Dɪᴇᴅ: October 10, 1797 in Richmond, Virginia

Aɢᴇ ᴀᴛ Dᴇᴀᴛʜ: 61

Fᴏᴜɴᴅɪɴɢ Dᴏᴄᴜᴍᴇɴᴛ Sɪɢɴᴇᴅ: The Declaration of Independence

Dɪᴅ Yᴏᴜ Kɴᴏw? Carter Braxton's mother died giving birth to him, so he was accidentally reported as dead, too.

DAVID BREARLY

BORN: June 11, 1745 in Trenton, New Jersey

DIED: August 16, 1790 in Trenton, New Jersey

AGE AT DEATH: 45

FOUNDING DOCUMENT SIGNED: The United States Constitution

DID YOU KNOW? In 1786, David Brearly helped write the prayer book of the Episcopal General Conference.

JACOB BROOM

BORN: October 17, 1752 in Wilmington, Delaware

DIED: April 15, 1810

AGE AT DEATH: 57

FOUNDING DOCUMENT SIGNED: The United States Constitution

DID YOU KNOW? In 1777, Jacob Broom, a surveyor, prepared the maps for George Washington for the Battle of Brandywine.

PIERCE BUTLER

BORN: July 11, 1744 in County Carlow, Ireland

DIED: February 15, 1822 in Philadelphia, Pennsylvania

AGE AT DEATH: 77

FOUNDING DOCUMENT SIGNED: The United States Constitution

DID YOU KNOW? Pierce Butler was a huge slaveholder and helped write the Fugitive Slave Clause, which required people to return escaped slaves to their rightful owner.

DANIEL CARROLL

BORN: July 22, 1730 in Upper Marlboro, Prince George's County, Maryland

DIED: May 7, 1796 in Forest Glen, Maryland

AGE AT DEATH: 65

FOUNDING DOCUMENT SIGNED: The United States Constitution

DID YOU KNOW? Daniel Carroll was one of only two Roman Catholics to sign the Constitution. (The other was Thomas Fitzsimons.)

SAMUEL CHASE

BORN: April 17, 1741 in Somerset County, Maryland

DIED: June 19, 1811 in Baltimore, Maryland

AGE AT DEATH: 70

FOUNDING DOCUMENT SIGNED: The Declaration of Independence

DID YOU KNOW? Samuel Chase's nickname was "Old Bacon Face."

ABRAHAM CLARK

BORN: February 15, 1726 in Elizabethtown, New Jersey

DIED: September 15, 1794 in New Jersey

AGE AT DEATH: 68

FOUNDING DOCUMENT SIGNED: The Declaration of Independence

DID YOU KNOW? Abraham Clark died from sunstroke.

GEORGE CLYMER

BORN: March 16, 1739 in Philadelphia, Pennsylvania

DIED: January 23, 1813 in Morrisville, Pennsylvania

AGE AT DEATH: 73

FOUNDING DOCUMENTS SIGNED: The Declaration of Independence, the United States Constitution

DID YOU KNOW? George Clymer was orphaned when he was only a year old.

JONATHAN DAYTON

BORN: October 16, 1760 in Elizabethtown, New Jersey

DIED: October 9, 1824 Elizabethtown, New Jersey

AGE AT DEATH: 63

POLITICAL PARTY: Pro–Administration

FOUNDING DOCUMENT SIGNED: The United States Constitution

DID YOU KNOW? Jonathan Dayton was charged with treason for lending money to Aaron Burr.

WILLIAM ELLERY

BORN: December 2, 1727 in Newport, Rhode Island

DIED: February 15, 1820 in Newport, Rhode Island

AGE AT DEATH: 92

FOUNDING DOCUMENT SIGNED: The Declaration of Independence

DID YOU KNOW? William Ellery's signature was second in size to John Hancock's on the United States Constitution.

WILLIAM FEW

Born: June 8, 1748 in Baltimore County, Maryland

Died: July 16, 1828 in Fishkill-on-Hudson, New York

Age at Death: 80

Founding Document Signed: The United States Constitution

Did You Know? William Few was the director of the Manhattan Bank—which is now Citigroup—for 10 years, 1801–1814.

THOMAS FITZSIMONS

Born: October, 1741 in County Wexford, Ireland

Died: August 26, 1811 in Philadelphia, Pennsylvania

Age at Death: 69

Founding Document Signed: The United States Constitution

Did You Know? Thomas Fitzsimons was one of only two Roman Catholics to sign the Constitution. (The other was Daniel Carroll.)

WILLIAM FLOYD

Born: December 17, 1734 in Brookhaven, New York

Died: August 4, 1821 in Westernville, New York

Age at Death: 86

Founding Document Signed: The Declaration of Independence

Did You Know? When William Floyd was 86, he had 6 slaves and 2 free blacks living with him in his house in Westernville, New York.

NICHOLAS GILMAN

Born: August 3, 1755 in Exeter, New Hampshire

Died: May 2, 1814 in Philadelphia, Pennsylvania

Age at Death: 58

Founding Document Signed: The United States Constitution

Did You Know? Nicholas Gilman's gravestone is cracked and crumbling, which is a true irony considering that his state, New Hampshire, is the Granite State.

NATHANIEL GORHAM

Born: May 27, 1738 in Charlestown, Massachusetts

Died: June 11, 1796 in Charlestown, Massachusetts

Age at Death: 58

Founding Document Signed: The United States Constitution

Did You Know? Nathaniel Gorham's wife, Mary Gye Maverick, was descended from royalty.

BUTTON GWINNETT

Born: 1735 in Gloucestershire, Great Britain

Died: May 19, 1777 in Savannah, Georgia

Age at Death: 42

Founding Document Signed: The Declaration of Independence

Did You Know? Button Gwinnett died from gunshots received in a duel with Lachlan McIntosh.

LYMAN HALL

Born: April 12, 1724 in Wallingford, Connecticut

Died: October 19, 1790 in Burke County, Georgia

Age at Death: 66

Founding Document Signed: The Declaration of Independence

Did You Know? Lyman Hall became a minister, but was fired when he argued with his congregation.

CORNELIUS HARNETT

Born: April 20, 1723 in Chowan County, North Carolina

Died: April 28, 1781 in Wilmington, North Carolina

Age at Death: 58

Founding Document Signed: The Declaration of Independence

Did You Know? Cornelius Harnett was crippled with gout and died after being captured, manhandled, and imprisoned by the British.

BENJAMIN HARRISON V

Born: April 5, 1726 in Charles City County, Virginia

Died: April 24, 1791 in Charles City County, Virginia

Age at Death: 65

Founding Document Signed: The Declaration of Independence

Did You Know? Benjamin Harrison V's son William Henry Harrison, and his grandson, Benjamin Harrison, were both elected president of the United States.

JOHN HART

BORN: Between 1706 and 1713 in Stonington, Connecticut

DIED: May 11, 1779 in Hunterdon County, New Jersey

AGE AT DEATH: Between 66 and 74

FOUNDING DOCUMENT SIGNED: The Declaration of Independence

DID YOU KNOW? From June 22–24, 1778, John Hart allowed 12,000 soldiers to live on his fields prior to the Battle of Monmouth.

JOSEPH HEWES

BORN: January 23, 1730 Princeton, New Jersey

DIED: November 10, 1779 in New Jersey

AGE AT DEATH: 49

FOUNDING DOCUMENT SIGNED: The Declaration of Independence

DID YOU KNOW? Every member of the Continental Congress attended Joseph Hewes' funeral.

THOMAS HEYWARD JR.

BORN: July 28, 1746 in St. Luke's Parish, South Carolina

DIED: March 6, 1809 in Old House, South Carolina

AGE AT DEATH: 62

FOUNDING DOCUMENT SIGNED: The Declaration of Independence

DID YOU KNOW? The opera *Porgy and Bess* is based on a novel, *Porgy*, written by one of Thomas Heyward Jr.'s descendants.

WILLIAM HOOPER

BORN: June 28, 1742 in Boston, Massachusetts

DIED: October 14, 1790 in North Carolina

AGE AT DEATH: 48

FOUNDING DOCUMENTS SIGNED: The Continental Association, the Declaration of Independence

DID YOU KNOW? William Hooper graduated from Harvard when he was only 18 years old.

STEPHEN HOPKINS

BORN: March 7, 1707 in Providence, Rhode Island

DIED: July 13, 1785 in Providence, Rhode Island

AGE AT DEATH: 78

FOUNDING DOCUMENT SIGNED: The Declaration of Independence

DID YOU KNOW? Stephen Hopkins was an astronomer and recorded the 1769 transit of Venus across the Sun.

SAMUEL HUNTINGTON

BORN: July 16, 1731 in Windham, Connecticut

DIED: January 5, 1796 in Norwich, Connecticut

AGE AT DEATH: 64

FOUNDING DOCUMENT SIGNED: The Declaration of Independence

DID YOU KNOW? Some people consider Samuel Huntington the true first president of the United States because he was president of Congress when the Articles of Confederation were signed.

JARED INGERSOLL

BORN: October 24, 1749 in New Haven, Connecticut

DIED: October 31, 1822 in Philadelphia, Pennsylvania

AGE AT DEATH: 73

FOUNDING DOCUMENT SIGNED: The United States Constitution

DID YOU KNOW? Jared Ingersoll's father was tarred and feathered by patriots because he supported King George and was against independence.

WILLIAM SAMUEL JOHNSON

BORN: October 7, 1727 in Stratford, Connecticut

DIED: November 14, 1819 in Stratford, Connecticut

AGE AT DEATH: 92

FOUNDING DOCUMENT SIGNED: The United States Constitution

DID YOU KNOW? When William Samuel Johnson visited British commander General Thomas Gage, he was arrested for communicating with the enemy.

JOHN LANGDON

BORN: June 26, 1741 in Portsmouth, New Hampshire

DIED: September 18, 1819 in Portsmouth, New Hampshire

AGE AT DEATH: 78

FOUNDING DOCUMENT SIGNED: The United States Constitution

DID YOU KNOW? John Langdon was the captain of a cargo ship at the age of 22.

FRANCIS LIGHTFOOT LEE

BORN: October 14, 1734 in Westmoreland County, Virginia

DIED: January 11, 1797 in Richmond County, Virginia

AGE AT DEATH: 62

FOUNDING DOCUMENT SIGNED: The Declaration of Independence

DID YOU KNOW? Francis Lightfoot Lee and his wife (and second cousin) Rebecca died 4 days apart.

FRANCIS LEWIS

BORN: March 21, 1713 in Llandaff, Wales

DIED: December 31, 1802 in Manhattan, New York

AGE AT DEATH: 89

FOUNDING DOCUMENT SIGNED: The Declaration of Independence

DID YOU KNOW? After being caught as a British spy in New York, Francis Lewis was sent to France (alive) in a box.

PHILIP LIVINGSTON

BORN: January 15, 1716 in Albany, New York

DIED: June 12, 1778 in York, Pennsylvania

AGE AT DEATH: 62

FOUNDING DOCUMENT SIGNED: The Declaration of Independence

DID YOU KNOW? Philip Livingston had dropsy, which we now know as edema, and died suddenly, probably from heart failure.

WILLIAM LIVINGSTON

BORN: November 30, 1723 in Albany, New York

DIED: July 25, 1790 in Elizabeth, New Jersey

AGE AT DEATH: 66

FOUNDING DOCUMENT SIGNED: The United States Constitution

DID YOU KNOW? William Livingston was a poet whose poem *Philosophic Solitude, or the Choice of a Rural Life* was very successful.

THOMAS LYNCH JR.

BORN: August 5, 1749 in Georgetown, South Carolina

DISAPPEARED: 1779 in the Atlantic Ocean

Age at Death: 29–30

Founding Document Signed: The Declaration of Independence

Did You Know? Thomas Lynch Jr. was lost at sea, and his body was never recovered.

JAMES McHENRY

Born: November 16, 1753 in Ballymena, Ireland

Died: May 3, 1816 Baltimore, Maryland

Age at Death: 62

Founding Document Signed: The United States Constitution

Did You Know? James McHenry became a doctor after studying under another Founder, Benjamin Rush.

THOMAS McKEAN

Born: March 19, 1734 in New London Township, Pennsylvania

Died: June 24, 1817 in Philadelphia, Pennsylvania

Age at Death: 83

Founding Document Signed: The Declaration of Independence

Did You Know? Thomas McKean always carried a gold-headed cane.

ARTHUR MIDDLETON

Born: March 21, 1742 in Charleston, South Carolina

Died: January 1, 1787 in Charleston, South Carolina

Age at Death: 44

Founding Document Signed: The Declaration of Independence

Did You Know? One of Arthur Middleton's descendants, actor Charles B. Middleton, played Ming the Merciless in the *Flash Gordon* movies of the 1930s.

LEWIS MORRIS

Born: April 8, 1726 in Morrisania, New York

Died: January 22, 1798 in Morrisania, New York

Age at Death: 71

Founding Document Signed: The Declaration of Independence

Did You Know? Lewis Morris signed the Declaration of Independence after saying, "Damn the consequences! Give me the pen!"

THOMAS NELSON JR.

BORN: December 26, 1738 in Yorktown, Virginia

DIED: January 4, 1789 in Hanover County, Virginia, United States

AGE AT DEATH: 50

FOUNDING DOCUMENT SIGNED: The Declaration of Independence

DID YOU KNOW? Thomas Nelson Jr.'s wife Lucy was a very talented harpsichordist.

WILLIAM PACA

BORN: October 31, 1740 in Baltimore, Maryland

DIED: October 23, 1799 in Queen Anne's County, Maryland

AGE AT DEATH: 58

FOUNDING DOCUMENT SIGNED: The Declaration of Independence

DID YOU KNOW? William Paca, although born in Maryland, may, or may not have been of Italian descent.

ROBERT TREAT PAINE

BORN: March 11, 1731 in Boston, Massachusetts

DIED: May 11, 1814 in Boston, Massachusetts

AGE AT DEATH: 83

FOUNDING DOCUMENT SIGNED: The Declaration of Independence

DID YOU KNOW? Robert Treat Paine was only 18 when he graduated from Harvard.

JOHN PENN

BORN: May 17, 1741 in Caroline County, Virginia

DIED: September 14, 1788 in Granville County, North Carolina

AGE AT DEATH: 47

FOUNDING DOCUMENT SIGNED: The Declaration of Independence

DID YOU KNOW? In 1936, North Carolina erected an historical highway marker in John Penn's honor, the first ever in the state.

GEORGE READ

BORN: September 18, 1733 in Cecil County, Maryland

DIED: September 21, 1798 in New Castle, Delaware

AGE AT DEATH: 65

FOUNDING DOCUMENTS SIGNED: The Declaration of Independence, the United States Constitution

DID YOU KNOW? George Read signed 3 of the founding documents of America, the 1774 Petition to the King, the Declaration of Independence, and the United States Constitution.

CAESAR RODNEY

BORN: October 7, 1728 in Kent County, Delaware

DIED: June 26, 1784 in Kent County, Delaware

AGE AT DEATH: 55

FOUNDING DOCUMENT SIGNED: The Declaration of Independence

DID YOU KNOW? As an adult, Caesar Rodney developed facial cancer and always wore a green scarf to hide his disfigurement.

GEORGE ROSS

BORN: May 10, 1730 in New Castle, Delaware

DIED: July 14, 1779 in Philadelphia, Pennsylvania

AGE AT DEATH: 49

FOUNDING DOCUMENT SIGNED: The Declaration of Independence

DID YOU KNOW? George Ross was Betsy Ross's uncle.

JOHN RUTLEDGE

BORN: September 17, 1739 in Charleston, South Carolina

DIED: July 23, 1800 in Charleston, South Carolina

AGE AT DEATH: 60

FOUNDING DOCUMENTS SIGNED: The Declaration of Independence, the United States Constitution

DID YOU KNOW? John Rutledge once tried to commit suicide by jumping into Charlestown Harbor.

JAMES SMITH

BORN: September 17, 1719 in Ulster, Ireland

DIED: July 11, 1806 in York, Pennsylvania

AGE AT DEATH: 86

FOUNDING DOCUMENT SIGNED: The Declaration of Independence

DID YOU KNOW? In 1805 a fire destroyed James Smith's office and papers, so very little accurate historical information about him survived.

RICHARD DOBBS SPAIGHT

BORN: March 25, 1758 in New Bern, North Carolina

DIED: September 6, 1802 in New Bern, North Carolina

AGE AT DEATH: 44

FOUNDING DOCUMENT SIGNED: The United States Constitution

DID YOU KNOW? Richard Dobbs Spaight was only 29 when he signed the United States Constitution and only 44 when he died from injuries sustained in a duel.

RICHARD STOCKTON

BORN: October 1, 1730 in Princeton, New Jersey

DIED: February 28, 1781 in Princeton, New Jersey

AGE AT DEATH: 50

FOUNDING DOCUMENT SIGNED: The Declaration of Independence

DID YOU KNOW? Richard Stockton died of cancer of the lip that spread to his throat.

THOMAS STONE

BORN: 1743 in Charles County, Maryland

DIED: October 5, 1787 Alexandria, Virginia

AGE AT DEATH: 43–44

FOUNDING DOCUMENT SIGNED: The Declaration of Independence

DID YOU KNOW? Although details are sketchy, it is reported that Thomas Stone's wife got sick from a smallpox inoculation that ultimately killed her several years later.

GEORGE TAYLOR

BORN: 1716 in Ireland

DIED: February 23, 1781 in Easton, Pennsylvania

AGE AT DEATH: 64–65

FOUNDING DOCUMENT SIGNED: The Declaration of Independence

DID YOU KNOW? George Taylor's ironworks company made cannon shells for the Continental Army.

MATTHEW THORNTON

BORN: 1714 in Limerick, Ireland

DIED: June 24, 1803 in Newburyport, Massachusetts

AGE AT DEATH: 88–89

Founding Document Signed: The Declaration of Independence

Did You Know? When Matthew Thornton's family immigrated to America from Ireland in 1718, they had no place to live when they arrived, so they stayed on the boat.

GEORGE WALTON

Born: 1749 in Cumberland County, Virginia

Died: February 2, 1804 in Augusta, Georgia

Age at Death: 54–55

Founding Document Signed: The Declaration of Independence

Did You Know? George Walton was captured by the British and held for 2 years after a cannonball hit him in the leg.

WILLIAM WHIPPLE

Born: January 14, 1730 in Kittery, Maine

Died: November 28, 1785 in Portsmouth, New Hampshire

Age at Death: 55

Founding Document Signed: The Declaration of Independence

Did You Know? William Whipple was one of the nine signers of the Declaration of Independence who were Freemasons.

WILLIAM WILLIAMS

Born: April 23, 1731 in Lebanon, Connecticut

Died: August 2, 1811 in Lebanon, Connecticut

Age at Death: 80

Founding Document Signed: The Declaration of Independence

Did You Know? During the Revolutionary War, William Williams would purchase supplies for the Continental Army with his own money.

HUGH WILLIAMSON

Born: December 5, 1735 in West Nottingham Township, Pennsylvania

Died: May 22, 1819 in New York City, New York

Age at Death: 83

Founding Document Signed: The United States Constitution

Did You Know? Hugh Williamson, a physician who was passionate about hygiene and diet, kept his soldiers free of disease for the 6 months they occupied the Dismal Swamp in North Carolina.

OLIVER WOLCOTT

BORN: November 20, 1726 in Windsor, Connecticut

DIED: December 1, 1797 in Farmington, Connecticut

AGE AT DEATH: 71

FOUNDING DOCUMENT SIGNED: The Declaration of Independence

DID YOU KNOW? When patriots stole the head of a King George statue as an act of rebellion (intending to impale it on a stake—it ended up being smuggled to England), Oliver Wolcott took the rest of the pieces of the statue, brought them home, melted them down, and formed the molten metal into bullets to be used to kill the British.

PART III

THE READING ROOM

A warm place ensconced in wood, lit by the glow of an oil lantern

Chapter 33
Check These Out

African Slavery In America by Thomas Paine

Note: This was originally published anonymously, and some Paine scholars contest that this is the work of Paine. The Thomas Paine National Historical Association has stated that "this is probably not written by Paine." The view of others, though, including the Constitution Society (constitution.org) is that this was indeed written by Paine. We include it for educational purposes, and because if it is ultimately a Paine essay, it provides insight into his thinking and moral foundation.

To Americans:

That some desperate wretches should be willing to steal and enslave men by violence and murder for gain, is rather lamentable than strange. But that many civilized, nay, Christianized people should approve, and be concerned in the savage practice, is surprising; and still persist, though it has been so often proved contrary to the light of nature, to every principle of Justice and Humanity, and even good policy, by a succession of eminent men, and several late publications.

Our Traders in MEN (an unnatural commodity!) must know the wickedness of the SLAVE-TRADE, if they attend to reasoning, or the dictates of their own hearts: and such as shun and stiffle all these, wilfully sacrifice Conscience, and the character of integrity to that golden idol.

The Managers the Trade themselves, and others testify, that many of these African nations inhabit fertile countries, are industrious farmers, enjoy plenty, and lived quietly, averse to war, before the Europeans debauched them with liquors, and bribing them against one another; and that these inoffensive people are brought into slavery, by stealing them, tempting Kings to sell subjects, which they can have no right to do, and hiring one tribe to war against another, in order to catch prisoners. By such wicked and inhuman ways the

English are said to enslave towards one hundred thousand yearly; of which thirty thousand are supposed to die by barbarous treatment in the first year; besides all that are slain in the unnatural ways excited to take them. So much innocent blood have the managers and supporters of this inhuman trade to answer for to the common Lord of all!

Many of these were not prisoners of war, and redeemed from savage conquerors, as some plead; and they who were such prisoners, the English, who promote the war for that very end, are the guilty authors of their being so; and if they were redeemed, as is alleged, they would owe nothing to the redeemer but what he paid for them.

They show as little reason as conscience who put the matter by with saying — "Men, in some cases, are lawfully made slaves, and why may not these?" So men, in some cases, are lawfully put to death, deprived of their goods, without their consent; may any man, therefore, be treated so, without any conviction of desert? Nor is this plea mended by adding — "They are set forth to us as slaves, and we buy them without farther inquiry, let the sellers see to it." Such man may as well join with a known band of robbers, buy their ill-got goods, and help on the trade; ignorance is no more pleadable in one case than the other; the sellers plainly own how they obtain them. But none can lawfully buy without evidence that they are not concurring with Men-Stealers; and as the true owner has a right to reclaim his goods that were stolen, and sold; so the slave, who is proper owner of his freedom, has a right to reclaim it, however often sold.

Most shocking of all is alledging the sacred scriptures to favour this wicked practice. One would have thought none but infidel cavillers would endeavour to make them appear contrary to the plain dictates of natural light, and the conscience, in a matter of common Justice and Humanity; which they cannot be. Such worthy men, as referred to before, judged otherways; Mr. Baxter declared, the Slave-Traders should be called Devils, rather than Christians; and that it is a heinous crime to buy them. But some say, "the practice was permitted to the Jews." To which may be replied,

1. The example of the Jews, in many things, may not be imitated by us; they had not only orders to cut off several nations altogether, but if they were obliged to war with others, and conquered them, to cut off every male; they were suffered to use polygamy and divorces, and other things utterly unlawful to us under clearer light.
2. The plea is, in a great measure, false; they had no permission to catch and enslave people who never injured them.

3. Such arguments ill become us, since the time of reformation came, under Gospel light. All distinctions of nations and privileges of one above others, are ceased; Christians are taught to account all men their neighbours; and love their neighbours as themselves; and do to all men as they would be done by; to do good to all men; and Man-stealing is ranked with enormous crimes. Is the barbarous enslaving our inoffensive neighbours, and treating them like wild beasts subdued by force, reconcilable with the Divine precepts! Is this doing to them as we would desire they should do to us? If they could carry off and enslave some thousands of us, would we think it just? — One would almost wish they could for once; it might convince more than reason, or the Bible.

As much in vain, perhaps, will they search ancient history for examples of the modern Slave-Trade. Too many nations enslaved the prisoners they took in war. But to go to nations with whom there is no war, who have no way provoked, without farther design of conquest, purely to catch inoffensive people, like wild beasts, for slaves, is an height of outrage against humanity and justice, that seems left by heathen nations to be practised by pretended Christian. How shameful are all attempts to colour and excuse it!

As these people are not convicted of forfeiting freedom, they have still a natural, perfect right to it; and the governments whenever they come should, in justice set them free, and punish those who hold them in slavery.

So monstrous is the making and keeping them slaves at all, abstracted from the barbarous usage they suffer, and the many evils attending the practice; as selling husbands away from wives, children from parents, and from each other, in violation of sacred and natural ties; and opening the way for adulteries, incests, and many shocking consequences, for all of which the guilty Masters must answer to the final Judge.

If the slavery of the parents be unjust, much more is their children's; if the parents were justly slaves, yet the children are born free; this is the natural, perfect right of all mankind; they are nothing but a just recompense to those who bring them up: And as much less is commonly spent on them than others, they have a right, in justice, to be proportionably sooner free.

Certainly, one may, with as much reason and decency, plead for murder, robbery, lewdness and barbarity, as for this practice. They are not more contrary to the natural dictates of conscience, and feeling of humanity; nay, they are all comprehended in it.

But the chief design of this paper is not to disprove it, which many have sufficiently done; but to entreat Americans to consider.

1. With what consistency, or decency they complain so loudly of attempts to enslave them, while they hold so many hundred thousands in slavery; and annually enslave many thousands more, without any pretence of authority, or claim upon them?

2. How just, how suitable to our crime is the punishment with which Providence threatens us? We have enslaved multitudes, and shed much innocent blood in doing it; and now are threatened with the same. And while other evils are confessed, and bewailed, why not this especially, and publicity; than which no other vice, if all others, has brought so much guilt on the land?

3. Whether, then, all ought not immediately to discontinue and renounce it, with grief and abhorrence? Should not every society bear testimony against it, and account obstinate persisters in it bad men, enemies to their country, and exclude them from fellowship; as they often do for much lesser faults?

4. The great Question may be — What should be done with those who are enslaved already? To turn the old and infirm free, would be injustice and cruelty; they who enjoyed the labours of the their better days should keep, and treat them humanely. As to the rest, let prudent men, with the assistance of legislatures, determine what is practicable for masters, and best for them. Perhaps some could give them lands upon reasonable rent, some, employing them in their labour still, might give them some reasonable allowances for it; so as all may have some property, and fruits of their labours at the own disposal, and be encouraged to industry; the family may live together, and enjoy the natural satisfaction of exercising relative affections and duties, with civil protection, and other advantages, like fellow men. Perhaps they might sometime form useful barrier settlements on the frontiers. Thus they may become interested in the public welfare, and assist in promoting it; instead of being dangerous, as now they are, should any enemy promise them a better condition.

5. The past treatment of Africans must naturally fill them with abhorrence of Christians; lead them to think our religion would make them more inhuman savages, if they embraced it; thus the gain of that trade has been pursued in oppositions of the redeemer's cause, and the happiness of men. Are we not, therefore, bound in duty to him and to them to repair these injuries, as far as possible, by taking some proper measure to instruct, not only the slaves here, but the Africans in their own countries? Primitive Christians, laboured always to spread the divine religion; and

this is equally our duty while there is an heathen nation: But what singular obligations are we under to these injured people!

These are the sentiments of JUSTICE AND HUMANITY.

DRINK UP! THE ALCOHOLIC BEVERAGES CONSUMED TWO DAYS BEFORE THE SIGNING OF THE DECLARATION OF INDEPENDENCE

According to addiction expert Stanton Peele, historical records indicate that the following alcoholic beverages were imbibed at a party two days before the signers signed the Declaration of Independence:

- 54 bottles of Madeira
- 60 bottles of claret
- 8 bottles of whiskey
- 22 bottles of porter
- 8 bottles of hard cider
- 12 bottles of beer
- 7 bowls of alcoholic punch

The Opening of the "Declaration of Independence"

IN CONGRESS, July 4, 1776.

The unanimous Declaration of the thirteen united States of America,

When in the Course of human events, it becomes necessary for one people to dissolve the political bands which have connected them with another, and to assume among the powers of the earth, the separate and equal station to which the Laws of Nature and of Nature's God entitle them, a decent respect to the opinions of mankind requires that they should declare the causes which impel them to the separation.

We hold these truths to be self-evident, that all men are created equal, that they are endowed by their Creator with certain unalienable Rights, that among these are Life, Liberty and the pursuit of Happiness.—That to secure these rights, Governments are instituted among Men, deriving their just powers from the consent of the governed, —That whenever any Form of Government becomes destructive of these ends, it is the Right of the People to alter or to abolish it, and to institute new Government, laying its foundation on such principles and organizing its powers in such form, as to them shall seem most likely to effect their Safety and Happiness. Prudence, indeed, will dictate that Governments long established should not be changed for light and transient causes; and accordingly all experience hath shewn, that mankind are more disposed to suffer, while evils are sufferable, than to right themselves by abolishing the forms to which they are accustomed. But when a long train of abuses and usurpations, pursuing invariably the same Object evinces a design to reduce them under absolute Despotism, it is their right, it is their duty, to throw off such Government, and to provide new Guards for their future security.—Such has been the patient sufferance of these Colonies; and such is now the necessity which constrains them to alter their former Systems of Government.

The British Response to the Declaration of Independence

This is hilarious in hindsight.

Essentially, King George, via his flunkies, talked to the colonists like they were children, describing their claim to be independent of the Crown as "extravagant" and "inadmissible," thus completely missing the point of the Declaration of Independence.

The king calls them "misguided," and "aggrieved," and hints that if they keep this up, they put at risk their freedom, property, and life.

The king says he'll consider revising his "royal Instructions" if his "Subjects" feel it impedes their "Freedom of Legislation," but then come the threats, accompanied by a warning that the colonists should "reflect seriously upon their . . . expectations."

About a month later, the king spoke to the British Parliament, essentially admitting things were definitely not going well for Britain in the nation's war with the United States.

Y'think?

Although the Congress, whom the misguided Americans suffer to direct their Opposition to a re-establishment of the constitutional Government of these Provinces, have disavowed every purpose of Reconciliation, not consonant with their extravagant and inadmissible Claim of Independency, the King's Commissioners think fit to declare, that they are equally desirous to confer with his Majesty's well-affected subjects, upon the Means of restoring the public Tranquility, and establishing a permanent Union with every Colony as a Part of the British Empire.

The King, being most graciously disposed to direct a Revision of such of his royal Instructions, as may be construed to lay an improper Restraint upon the Freedom of Legislation, in any of his Colonies. And to concur in the Revival of all Acts by which his Subjects there may think themselves aggrieved; it is recommended to the Inhabitants at large, to reflect seriously upon their present Condition and Expectations, and to judge for themselves, whether it be more consistent with their Honour and Happiness to offer up their Lives as a Sacrifice to the unjust and precarious Cause in which they are engaged, or to return to their Allegiance, accept the Blessings of Peace, and be secured in a free Enjoyment of their Liberty and Properties, upon the true Principles of the Constitution.

Given at New-York, the 19th of Sept. 1776

HOWE. W. HOWE

By Command of their Excellencies.

HEN. STRACHEY

George Washington's Inaugural Address of April 30, 1789

The First Presidential Inaugural Address of the United States of America

A Transcription Taken from the Original Document in the National Archives

1,432 words

Fellow Citizens of the Senate and the House of Representatives.

Among the vicissitudes incident to life, no event could have filled me with greater anxieties than that of which the notification was transmitted by your order, and received on the fourteenth day of the present month. On the one hand, I was summoned by my Country, whose voice I can never hear but with veneration and love, from a retreat which I had chosen with the fondest predilection, and, in my flattering hopes, with an immutable decision, as the asylum of my declining years: a retreat which was rendered every day more necessary as well as more dear to me, by the addition of habit to inclination, and of frequent interruptions in my health to the gradual waste committed on it by time. On the other hand, the magnitude and difficulty of the trust to which the voice of my Country called me, being sufficient to awaken in the wisest and most experienced of her citizens, a distrustful scrutiny into his qualifications, could not but overwhelm with dispondence, one, who, inheriting inferior endowments from nature and unpractised in the duties of civil administration, ought to be peculiarly conscious of his own deficiencies. In this conflict of emotions, all I dare aver, is, that it has been my faithful study to collect my duty from a just appreciation of every circumstance, by which it might be affected. All I dare hope, is, that, if in executing this task I have been too much swayed by a grateful remembrance of former instances, or by an affectionate sensibility to this transcendent proof, of the confidence of my fellow-citizens; and have thence too little consulted my incapacity as well as disinclination for the weighty and untried cares before me; my error will be palliated by the motives which misled me, and its consequences be judged by my Country, with some share of the partiality in which they originated.

Such being the impressions under which I have, in obedience to the public summons, repaired to the present station; it would be peculiarly improper to omit in this first official Act, my fervent supplications to that Almighty Being who rules over the Universe, who presides in the Councils of Nations, and whose providential aids can supply every human defect, that his benediction may consecrate to the liberties and happiness of the People of the United States, a Government instituted by themselves for these essential purposes: and may enable every instrument employed in its administration to execute with success, the functions allotted to his charge. In tendering this homage to the Great Author of every public and private good I assure myself that it expresses your sentiments not less than my own; nor those of my fellow-citizens at large, less than either. No People can be bound to acknowledge and adore the invisible hand, which conducts the Affairs of men more than the People of the United States. Every step, by which they have advanced to the character of an independent nation, seems to have been distinguished by some token of providential agency. And in the important revolution just accomplished in the system of their United Government, the tranquil deliberations and voluntary consent of so many distinct communities, from which the event has resulted, cannot be compared with the means by which most Governments have been established, without some return of pious gratitude along with an humble anticipation of the future blessings which the past seem to presage. These reflections, arising out of the present crisis, have forced themselves too strongly on my mind to be suppressed. You will join with me I trust in thinking, that there are none under the influence of which, the proceedings of a new and free Government can more auspiciously commence.

By the article establishing the Executive Department, it is made the duty of the President "to recommend to your consideration, such measures as he shall judge necessary and expedient." The circumstances under which

I now meet you, will acquit me from entering into that subject, farther than to refer to the Great Constitutional Charter under which you are assembled; and which, in defining your powers, designates the objects to which your attention is to be given. It will be more consistent with those circumstances, and far more congenial with the feelings which actuate me, to substitute, in place of a recommendation of particular measures, the tribute that is due to the talents, the rectitude, and the patriotism which adorn the characters selected to devise and adopt them. In these honorable qualifications, I behold the surest pledges, that as on one side, no local prejudices, or attachments; no seperate views, nor party animosities, will misdirect the comprehensive and equal eye which ought to watch over this great assemblage of communities and interests: so, on another, that the foundations of our National policy will be laid in the pure and immutable principles of private morality; and the pre-eminence of a free Government, be exemplified by all the attributes which can win the affections of its Citizens, and command the respect of the world.

I dwell on this prospect with every satisfaction which an ardent love for my Country can inspire: since there is no truth more thoroughly established, than that there exists in the economy and course of nature, an indissoluble union between virtue and happiness, between duty and advantage, between the genuine maxims of an honest and magnanimous policy, and the solid rewards of public prosperity and felicity: Since we ought to be no less persuaded that the propitious smiles of Heaven, can never be expected on a nation that disregards the eternal rules of order and right, which Heaven itself has ordained: And since the preservation of the sacred fire of liberty, and the destiny of the Republican model of Government, are justly considered as deeply, perhaps as finally staked, on the experiment entrusted to the hands of the American people.

Besides the ordinary objects submitted to your care, it will remain with your judgment to decide, how far an exercise of the occasional power delegated by the Fifth article of the Constitution is rendered expedient at the present juncture by the nature of objections which have been urged against the System, or by the degree of inquietude which has given birth to them. Instead of undertaking particular recommendations on this subject, in which I could be guided by no lights derived from official opportunities, I shall again give way to my entire confidence in your discernment and pursuit of the public good: For I assure myself that whilst you carefully avoid every alteration which might endanger the benefits of an United and effective Government, or wh ich ought to await the future lessons of experience; a reverence for the characteristic rights of freemen, and a regard for the public harmony, will sufficiently influence your deliberations on the question how far the former can be more impregnably fortified, or the latter be safely and advantageously promoted.

To the preceeding observations I have one to add, which will be most properly addressed to the House of Representatives. It concerns myself, and will therefore be as brief as possible. When I was first honoured with a call into the Service of my Country, then on the eve of an arduous struggle for its liberties, the light in which I contemplated my duty required that I should renounce every pecuniary compensation. From this resolution I have in no instance departed. And being still under the impressions which produced it, I must decline as inapplicable to myself, any share in the personal emoluments, which may be indispensably included in a permanent provision for the Executive Department; and must accordingly pray that the pecuniary estimates for the Station in which I am placed, may, during my continuance in it, be limited to such actual expenditures as the public good may be thought to require.

Having thus imported to you my sentiments, as they have been awakened by the occasion which brings us together, I shall take my present leave; but not without resorting once more to the benign parent of the human race, in humble supplication that since he has been pleased to favour the American people, with opportunities for deliberating in perfect tranquility, and dispositions for deciding with unparelleled unanimity on a form of Government, for the security of their Union, and the advancement of their happiness; so his divine blessing may be equally conspicuous in the enlarged views, the temperate consultations, and the wise measures on which the success of this Government must depend.

George Washington's Second Inaugural Address

Philadelphia, March 4, 1793

135 words

Fellow Citizens: I am again called upon by the voice of my country to execute the functions of its Chief Magistrate. When the occasion proper for it shall arrive, I shall endeavor to express the high sense I entertain of this distinguished honor, and of the confidence which has been reposed in me by the people of united America. Previous to the execution of any official act of the President the Constitution requires an oath of office. This oath I am now about to take, and in your presence: That if it shall be found during my administration of the Government I have in any instance violated willingly or knowingly the injunctions thereof, I may (besides incurring constitutional punishment) be subject to the upbraidings of all who are now witnesses of the present solemn ceremony.

The Bill of Rights: Take 2

The Bill of Rights—the first 10 Amendments to the United States Constitution—is a cornerstone American document that codifies specific inalienable rights belonging to every American citizen.

The First is certainly the Most Famous, and, to many, the Most Important Amendment:

> Congress shall make no law respecting an establishment of religion, or prohibiting the free exercise thereof; or abridging the freedom of speech, or of the press; or the right of the people peaceably to assemble, and to petition the government for a redress of grievances.

These 45 words have it all:
- Freedom of religion
- Freedom of speech
- Freedom of the press
- Freedom of assembly
- Freedom to petition the government

Yes, Americans can worship, or not; say what they want, print what they want, assemble anywhere they want, and complain to their government. In a sense, this Amendment concisely sums up what it means to be an American.

But this monumental, historic declaration of liberty and rights wasn't always the First in the Bill of Rights. Believe it or not, the original First Amendment in the first draft of the Bill of Rights was not in the least concerned with liberty:

> After the first enumeration required by the first article of the Constitution, there shall be one Representative for every thirty thousand, until the number shall amount to one hundred, after which the proportion shall be so regulated by Congress, that there shall be not less than one hundred Representatives, nor less than one Representative for every forty thousand persons, until the number of Representatives shall amount to two hundred; after which the proportion shall be so regulated by Congress, that there shall not be less than two hundred Representatives, nor more than one Representative for every fifty thousand persons.

And it gets worse.

The Second Amendment, which is the most argued about, the most contentious, the most loved, and the most hated Amendment, wasn't always the Second Amendment. This is the text of what many American gun rights advocates believe should have been listed first:

> A well regulated Militia, being necessary to the security of a free state, the right of the people to keep and bear Arms, shall not be infringed.

However, in the first draft of the Bill of Rights, this was the original Second Amendment:

> No law, varying the compensation for the services of the Senators and Representatives, shall take effect, until an election of Representatives shall have intervened.

A payroll amendment? Really?

But since the Founders certainly knew what they were doing, it wasn't long before it was acknowledged that the first Bill of Rights needed a new draft before it was carved in stone (er, scratched onto parchment, actually). And it didn't take much. They cut the first 2 Amendments and, voila! The Bill of Rights we know and love. (Also see "What Do the 27 Amendments to the Constitution Do?")

Excerpt from Patrick Henry's "Give Me Liberty or Give Me Death!" Speech

This speech was delivered by Patrick Henry on March 23, 1775, in St. John's Church in Richmond, Virginia. It served as the catalyst to enlist Virginia troops in the Revolutionary War. This excerpt is from the conclusion of the speech when Henry issues his immortal proclamation.

The war is inevitable and let it come! I repeat it, sir, let it come. It is in vain, sir, to extenuate the matter. Gentlemen may cry, Peace, Peace but there is no peace. The war is actually begun! The next gale that sweeps from the north will bring to our ears the clash of resounding arms! Our brethren are already in the field! Why stand we here idle? What is it that gentlemen wish? What would they have? Is life so dear, or peace so sweet, as to be purchased at the price of chains and slavery? Forbid it, Almighty God! I know not what course others may take; but as for me, give me liberty or give me death!

CHAPTER 34
THE ULTIMATE FOUNDING
FATHERS QUIZ

Are you now Founders-test-worthy? Can you answer these questions? Good luck!

1. Which Founding Father proclaimed, "I am murdered!"
    a. George Washington
    b. George Mason
    c. George Wythe
    d. Rufus King

2. Who was known as the American Fabius?
    a. Thomas Jefferson
    b. Elbridge Gerry
    c. Rufus King
    d. George Washington

3. Which Founding Father invented the swivel chair?
    a. Richard Henry Lee
    b. John Dickinson
    c. Thomas Jefferson
    d. John Hancock

4. Who was the only clergyman to sign the Declaration of Independence?
    a. John Witherspoon
    b. John Adams
    c. John Dickinson
    d. John Marshall

5. Which Founding Father was in charge of the construction of the Erie Canal?
    a. James Monroe
    b. Benjamin Franklin

c. Samuel Adams

d. Gouverneur Morris

6. Which Founding Father said "Give me liberty or give me death!"?
    a. Thomas Jefferson
    b. Thomas Paine
    c. Patrick Henry
    d. John Jay

7. Which Founding Father administered the oath of office to George Washington?
    a. James Madison
    b. Robert Morris
    c. Robert R. Livingston
    d. William Paterson

8. Which Founding Father entered Harvard when he was only 14 years old?
    a. William Paterson
    b. George Wythe
    c. Charles Cotesworth Pinckney
    d. Charles Pinckney

9. Which Founding Father put forth a proposal that United States Senators serve without pay?
    a. Thomas Jefferson
    b. Charles Cotesworth Pinckney
    c. Benjamin Rush
    d. Roger Sherman

10. Which founding Father had 15 children with 2 wives?
    a. James Madison
    b. James Monroe
    c. John Jay
    d. Roger Sherman

11. Who was the only Founder who went on to become president who did not have a college degree?
    a. George Washington
    b. Thomas Jefferson
    c. John Adams
    d. James Madison

12. Who brought French fries to the United States?
    a. Thomas Jefferson
    b. Benjamin Franklin
    c. Richard R. Livingston
    d. James Wilson

13. Which Founding Father is responsible for coining the words "armature" and "conductor"?
    a. Frances Hopkinson
    b. Charles Carroll of Carrollton
    c. Benjamin Franklin
    d. John Witherspoon

14. Which Founding Father edited the Bible to remove all the supernatural stuff?
    a. John Witherspoon
    b. John Marshall
    c. Roger Sherman
    d. Thomas Jefferson

15. Which Founding Father once lost $300,000 that was supposed to be used to pay soldiers?
    a. Charles Pinckney
    b. William Blount
    c. Charles Carroll of Carrollton
    d. George Mason

16. Which Founding Father can we thank for the term "gerrymandering"?
    a. Robert Morris
    b. Francis Hopkinson
    c. Elbridge Gerry
    d. John Adams

17. Which Founding Father invented the Bellarmonic?
    a. Benjamin Franklin
    b. Francis Hopkinson
    c. Thomas Jefferson
    d. James Monroe

18. Which Founding Father wanted Virginia to secede from the Union if the Bill of Rights was not ratified?
    a. Richard Henry Lee
    b. Robert R. Livingston

c. George Washington

d. Elbridge Gerry

19. Which Founding Father built a steamboat with Robert Fulton which promptly sank in the Seine on its maiden voyage?
a. Thomas Paine
b. Thomas Jefferson
c. Gouverneur Morris
d. Robert. R. Livingston

20. Which Founding Father, even to this day, is the longest serving chief justice in Supreme Court history?
a. John Marshall
b. George Wythe
c. John Witherspoon
d. Charles Cotesworth Pinckney

21. Which Founding Father called politicians "babblers"?
a. Charles Pinckney
b. Francis Hopkinson
c. George Mason
d. James Madison

22. Which Founding Father served time in a debtor's prison?
a. Robert R. Livingston
b. Robert Morris
c. James Wilson
d. Richard Henry Lee

23. Which Founding Father said, "The federal government—I deny their power to make paper money a legal tender."?
a. George Washington
b. Thomas Jefferson
c. John Adams
d. James Madison

24. How old was John Adams when he started smoking?
a. 8
b. 9
c. 10
d. He never smoked.

25. Which Founding Father never owned a single slave yet was against abolition, believing it would cause a ruckus?
    a. George Mason
    b. James Madison
    c. John Witherspoon
    d. John Adams

Match the quote from the left column with the Founding Father who said it from the right column.

_____ 26. "To prevent crimes, is the noblest end and aim of criminal jurisprudence. To punish them, is one of the means necessary for the accomplishment of this noble end and aim."	a. John Marshall
_____ 27. "Be at war with your vices, at peace with your neighbors, and let every new year find you a better man."	b. John Adams
_____ 28. "The education of children is a matter of vast importance and highly deserving of our most serious attention. The prosperity of our country is intimately connected with it; for without morals, there can be no order, and without knowledge, no genuine liberty."	c. Thomas Jefferson
_____ 29. "It is emphatically the province and duty of the judicial department to say what the law is. If two laws conflict with each other, the courts must decide on the operation of each. This is of the very essence of judicial duty."	d. Benjamin Franklin
_____ 30. "Freedom can exist only in the society of knowledge. Without learning, men are incapable of knowing their rights."	e. George Washington
_____ 31. "In every country and in every age, the priest has been hostile to liberty. He is always in alliance with the despot, abetting his abuses in return for protection to his own. It is error alone that needs the support of government. Truth can stand by itself."	f. James Wilson

_____ 32. "This magistrate is not the king. The people are the king."	g. George Mason
_____ 33. "It is contrary to the principles of reason and justice that any should be compelled to contribute to the maintenance of a church with which their consciences will not permit them to join, and from which they can derive no benefit; for remedy whereof, and that equal liberty as well religious as civil, may be universally extended to all the good people of this commonwealth."	h. Gouverneur Morris
_____ 34. "We must take human nature as we find it, perfection falls not to the share of mortals."	i. William Paterson
_____ 35. "The government of the United States is not, in any sense, founded on the Christian religion."	j. Benjamin Rush

Match the Founding Father from the left column with their spouse from the right column.

_____ 36. John Witherspoon	a. Rachel Bird
_____ 37. James Wilson	b. Abigail Smith
_____ 38. Charles Cotesworth Pinckney	c. Martha Custis
_____ 39. George Mason	d. Elizabeth Montgomery
_____ 40. George Washington	e. Deborah Read
_____ 41. Thomas Jefferson	f. Elizabeth Taliaferro
_____ 42. John Adams	g. Sarah Brent
_____ 43. Benjamin Franklin	h. Mary Ambler
_____ 44. George Wythe	i. Martha Skelton
_____ 45. John Marshall	j. Sarah Middleton
_____ 46. James Madison	k. Eliza Kortright
_____ 47. Alexander Hamilton	l. Sarah Livingston
_____ 48. James Monroe	m. Elizabeth Schuyler
_____ 49. Patrick Henry	n. Sarah Shelton
_____ 50. John Jay	o. Dolley Todd

ANSWERS TO THE ULTIMATE FOUNDING FATHERS QUIZ

1. b	2. d	3. c	4. a	5. d
6. c	7. c	8. a	9. b	10. d
11. a	12. a	13. c	14. d	15. b
16. c	17. b	18. a	19. d	20. a
21. c	22. b	23. b	24. a	25. d
26. f	27. d	28. i	29. a	30. j
31. c	32. h	33. g	34. e	35. b
36. d	37. a	38. j	39. g	40. c
41. 1	42. b	43. e	44. f	45. h
46. o	47. m	48. k	49. n	50. l

NOTES

1. Letter to John Augustine Washington, Philadelphia, June 20, 1775
2. Stephen Spignesi, *Grover Cleveland's Rubber Jaw*
3. Peter Henriques, *The Death of George Washington: He Died As He Lived.* Charlottesville, Virginia: University of Virginia Press, 2002.
4. Marvin Kitman, *The Making of the President 1789: The Unauthorized Campaign Biography.* New York: Grove/Atlantic, 2007.
5. August 15, 1786 letter to John Jay
6. Ibid.
7. Ibid.
8. Letter to the members of the New Church in Baltimore, January 27, 1793
9. Letter to the United Baptist Chamber of Virginia, May 1789
10. *Federalist*, No. 15
11. Address at the Hamilton Club, January 11, 1922
12. *Alexander Hamilton, The Farmer Refuted*, February 23, 1775
13. Letter to John Laurens, December, 1779
14. *Alexander Hamilton, The Farmer Refuted*, February 23, 1775
15. Speech at the Constitutional Convention, June 22, 1787
16. *Federalist* No 6, "Concerning Dangers from Dissensions Between the States," *Independent Journal*, November 14, 1787
17. Letter to James A. Bayard, April 16, 1802
18. Speech at the Constitutional Convention, June 22, 1787
19. *The Federalist*, 69, 1788
20. "Hamilton and History: Are They in Sync?" *The New York Times*, Jennifer Schuessler, April 10, 2016
21. *Canons of Conduct*
22. Stephen Spignesi, *Grover Cleveland's Rubber Jaw.* New York: Perigree, 2012
23. November 4, 1826 Letter to Samuel Harrison Smith
24. Thomas Jefferson did not sign the Constitution. He was in France at the time.
25. Letter to the Baptists of Danbury, Connecticut, 1802

26. Speech to the Virginia Baptists, 1808
27. Letter to Mathew Carey, November 11, 1816
28. Letter to Horatio Spofford, 1814
29. Letter to John Adams, 1813
30. Letter to Dr. Benjamin Waterhouse, October 13, 1815
31. Letter to Francis Adrian Van der Kemp, March 22, 1812
32. Letter to Peter Carr, August 10, 1787
33. Letter to Robert R. Livingston, April 18, 1803
34. Letter to Madison, 1789
35. 1814 Letter to John Taylor
36. Spignesi, *Grover Cleveland's Rubber Jaw*
37. September 1776 letter to a friend
38. Letter to Abigail Adams, July 3, 1776
39. These were John Adams' last words. He was wrong. Jefferson had already died.
40. Article 11 of the Treaty of Tripoli, 1797
41. 1770, Boston Massacre Trial
42. *Argument in Defense of the British Soldiers in the Boston Massacre Trials*, December 4, 1770
43. Ibid.
44. Letter to Dr. Price, April 8, 1785
45. July 7, 1775 Letter to Abigail Adams
46. Letter to John Taylor, 1814
47. John Adams, *A Dissertation on the Canon and Feudal Law*
48. Letter to Abigail Adams, July 3, 1776
49. *Poor Richard's Almanack*
50. *The Autobiography of Benjamin Franklin*
51. Notes prior to the 1787 Constitutional Convention
52. The Treaty of Paris ended the Revolutionary War and is considered one of the documents establishing the United States as a sovereign nation
53. "Chess and Benjamin Franklin: His Pioneering Contributions" by John McCrary
54. Benjamin Franklin, *The Autobiography of Benjamin Franklin*, 1793
55. Benjamin Franklin, *Poor Richard's Almanack*
56. *The Autobiography of Benjamin Franklin*
57. *Poor Richard's Almanack*
58. Benjamin Franklin, *The Way to Wealth*
59. Benjamin Franklin, *Silence Dogood, The Busy-Body, and Early Writings*

60. Letter to Richard Price, October 9, 1780
61. Letter to the London Packet, June 3, 1772
62. Speech at the Constitutional Convention, September 17, 1787
63. Letter to Francis Hopkinson, December 24, 1782
64. July 17, 1785 letter to R. H. Lee
65. Spignesi, *Grover Cleveland's Rubber Jaw*
66. Eulogy for James Madison, 1836
67. *The Autobiography of Benjamin Rush, His Travels Through Life Together With His Commonplace Book for 1789-1813*, Princeton University Press, 1948
68. The James Madison Papers, March 29, 1792.
69. Speech to the Constitutional Convention, July 11, 1787
70. Ibid.
71. "Vices of the Political System of the United States," April 1787
72. *National Gazette*, 1792
73. Speech to the Virginia Convention, June 6, 1788
74. Letter to Thomas Jefferson, October 1788
75. Speech to the Virginia Convention, December 2, 1829
76. 1819, *Writings*, 8:432
77. Letter to Albert Picket, September 1821
78. *The Federalist* No. 51, February 6, 1788
79. 1793
80. *The Federalist Papers. Federalist No. 2*
81. www.cia.gov
82. June 26, 1796 letter from George Washington to Alexander Hamilton
83. March 15, 1786 letter to Stephen Rumbold Lushington
84. *The Federalist Papers*, Federalist No. 4
85. Jay expressed this lovely sentiment to his wife Sarah Livingston Jay in a July 21, 1776 letter when he was away working on the cause of American independence.
86. *The Federalist Papers,* Federalist No. 64, March 5, 1788
87. Reportedly said at the Second Constitutional Convention, 1787.
88. "An Eulogy On the Life and Character of James Monroe, Fifth President of the United States," by John Adams, August 5, 1831
89. Said in conversation with his daughter Eliza in France
90. First Inaugural Address, March 4, 1817
91. State of the Union Address, November 16, 1818
92. Ibid.

93. Speech in the Virginia State Convention, November 2, 1829
94. *Common Sense,* 1776
95. Writing Paine's obituary in the *New York Evening Post*
96. "The Philosophy of Paine"
97. Said to his law partner Billy Herndon
98. http://allthingsliberty.com/2013/03/thomas-paines-inflated-numbers/
99. "Thomas Paine's Remains Are Still a Bone of Contention," April 1, 2001
100. *The Age of Reason*
101. *The Rights of Man,* 1791
102. *The American Crisis,* 1776
103. Ibid.
104. *Common Sense,* 1776
105. A variant of this quote was echoed by Benjamin Franklin
106. *Rights of Man,* 1791
107. *The American Crisis,* No. 1, December 19, 1776
108. *Common Sense,* 1776
109. *Speech in St. John's Church, Richmond, Virginia, March 23, 1775*
110. Letter to Daniel Webster
111. Speech at the Virginia Ratifying Convention, June 12, 1788
112. Speech to the Virginia Ratifying Convention, June 5, 1788
113. Religious Tolerance, 1766
114. Speech to the Virginia Ratifying Convention, June 5, 1788
115. April 30, 1776 letter to Samuel Cooper
116. Ibid.
117. *The Boston Gazette,* October 14, 1771
118. Letter to Samuel Cooper, April 30, 1776
119. Letter to James Warren, October 24, 1780
120. August 1, 1776 speech in Philadelphia
121. *The Boston Gazette,* 1781
122. *The Rights of the Colonists,* 1772
123. "The Rights of the Colonists," 1771
124. Instructions to Boston's Representatives, May 15, 1764
125. Boston Massacre Oration, March 5, 1774
126. Reverend Dr. Thatcher, Eulogy for John Hancock
127. Boston Massacre Oration, March 5, 1774
128. Ibid.
129. Letter from John Hancock announcing the Declaration of Independence, July 6, 1776

130. Boston Massacre Oration, March 5, 1774
131. Ibid.
132. Said at the Constitutional Convention of 1787
133. Gen. Marcus J. Wright in *William Blount: Some Account of the Life and Services of William Blount, an Officer of the Revolutionary Army, Member of the Continental Congress, and of the Convention which Framed the Constitution of the United States, also Governor of the Territory South of the Ohio River, and Senator in Congress U. S. 1783-1797*
134. Letter to unnamed friend about leaving North Carolina
135. Letter to Joseph Martin, June 16, 1791
136. Letter to Governor John Sevier, May 31, 1793
137. Letter to Henry Graves, September 15, 1765
138. *Charles Carroll: American Cicero*, Lecture by Dr. Brad Birzer, August 25, 2011
139. *John H. B. Latrobe and His Times, 1803-1891* by John E. Semmes, Baltimore, Maryland: The Waverly Press, 1917
140. Letter to Alexander Hamilton, April 18, 1800
141. Letter to Walter Graves, August 15, 1774
142. *The Life of Charles Carroll of Carrollton, 1737-1832*, G. P. Putnam's Sons, 1898
143. Letter to Henry Graves, September 15, 1765
144. Letter to his mother, August 12, 1760
145. Letter to Henry Graves, September 15, 1765
146. "The Liberty Song," 1768
147. Charles J Stillé, *The Life and Times of John Dickinson, 1732-1808*,
148. Letter to Dr. Joseph Bringhurst, February 24, 1808
149. Charles J Stillé, *The Life and Times of John Dickinson, 1732-1808*,
150. Letters from a Farmer in Pennsylvania, Letter 1
151. Ibid.
152. Letters from a Farmer in Pennsylvania, Letter 12
153. August 13, 1787 Speech at the Constitutional Convention
154. Ibid.
155. Said at The Debates in the Several State Conventions on the Adoption of the Federal Constitution, 1787
156. Gerry refused to sign the United States Constitution but was present at its signing
157. Annals of Congress 1:729-731

158. Debate in the House of Representatives about the 2nd Amendment, August 20, 1789

159. Speech to the Constitutional Convention, May 31, 1787

160. Ibid.

161. Ibid.

162. Letter to John Adams, November 23, 1783

163. Ibid.

164. Letter to Samuel and John Adams, July 21-22, 1776

165. Letter to Frances Hopkinson, June 4, 1779

166. *The Miscellaneous Essays and Occasional Writings of Francis Hopkinson, Esq.*

167. Ibid.

168. *The American Federalist.*

169. John Adams, Letter to Abigail Adams, July 7, 1774

170. King George

171. William Pierce at the Constitutional Convention

172. *The American Federalist.*

173. Letter to Henry Knox, March 13, 1785

174. Notes of Rufus King in the Federal Convention of 1787

175. Said amidst a crowd of free blacks on the Senate floor during a debate about the Missouri Compromise

176. "Resolution for Independence to the Second Continental Congress"

177. University of Groningen

178. John Adams

179. Letters of a Federal Farmer, 1787

180. Ibid.

181. Ibid.

182. Letter to Samuel Adams, 1787

183. Speech before the Second Continental Congress, June, 1776

184. Speech at the Louisiana State Capitol Building at the signing of the Louisiana Purchase Treaty, April 30, 1803

185. Commenting on Napoleon's quest for world conquest and the Louisiana Purchase

186. Letter to Rufus King, January 25, 1802 on the death of Alexander Hamilton in a duel

187. Letter to Rufus King, April 10, 1802

188. Letter to Rufus King, June 1802

189. McCulloch v. Maryland, 1819

190. John Randolph, *John Randolph of Roanoke, 1773–1833*

191. Marbury v. Madison, 1803
192. Osborn v. Bank of the United States, 1824
193. Cohens v. Virginia, 1821
194. McCulloch v. Maryland, 1819
195. Ibid.
196. The Trial of Aaron Burr, 1807
197. McCulloch v. Maryland, 1819
198. Speech at Virginia Ratifying Convention, June 17, 1788
199. July 18, 1763 letter to Alexander Henderson
200. October 14, 1775 letter to George Washington
201. Virginia Bill of Rights, 1776
202. Ibid.
203. Ibid.
204. Letter to London Merchants, June 6, 1766. He signed it "A Virginia Planter"
205. Ibid.
206. From the first draft of George Mason's *Virginia Declaration of Rights*, May 20-26, 1776, the model for the Bill of Rights amended to The United States Constitution
207. February 5, 1811 letter to Robert Walsh
208. He got this one for delivering 173 speeches—more than anyone else—at the Constitutional Convention
209. *Gouverneur Morris*, Boston, Mass.: Houghton Mifflin, 1892
210. James Madison, Report on Gouverneur Morris' Address to the Federal Constitutional Convention, 1787
211. Gouverneur Morris's half-brother, Lewis Morris was a signer of the Declaration of Independence
212. Speech at the Constitutional Convention, 1787
213. May 23, 1803 letter to John Dickinson
214. The Madison Debates, July 2, 1787
215. Debate at the Constitutional Convention, August 1787
216. Oration on the Death of George Washington, 1799
217. "On Prejudice," c. 1805
218. "On Patriotism," 1805
219. Righteousness Establisheth a Nation, 1780
220. Letter to Alexander Martin, July 20, 1782
221. Williams Pierce, *Character Sketches of Delegates to the Federal Convention*, 1787

222. Charles Rappleye, *Robert Morris: Financier of the American Revolution*

223. Ibid.

224. Letter to Alexander Martin, July 20, 1782

225. Ibid.

226. Letter to the President of Congress, July 29, 1782

227. Ibid.

228. May 24, 1800

229. Leonard B. Rosenberg, "William Paterson: New Jersey's Nation-Maker (1745-1806)"

230. "On Education," c. 1793-1795

231. Van Horne's Lessee v. Dorrance, April 1795

232. Ibid.

233. United States v. Smith, 1806

234. First draft of the First Amendment, presented at the Philadelphia Convention, May 29, 1787

235. Engraved on his tombstone

236. Pinckney reportedly said this when British soldiers who were holding him prisoner tried to persuade him to abandon the fight for American freedom

237. Pinckney's response when asked for a bribe from France

238. Letter to Alexander Hamilton, January 23, 1800

239. Letter to Alexander Hamilton, July 12, 1799

240. Elliot's Debates, IV

241. Speech to the Constitutional Convention, 1787

242. Elliot's Debates, IV

243. Letter to John Adams, October 22, 1797

244. Letter to Elias Boudinot, July 9, 1788

245. Dagobert D. Runes, ed., "Education Agreeable to a Republican Form of Government," *The Selected Writings of Benjamin Rush*, New York: Philosophical Library, 1947.

246. Letter to William Peterkin, 1784

247. *A Moral and Physical Thermometer*, 1789

248. *The Selected Writings of Benjamin Rush*, 1947

249. Letter to Thomas Jefferson, October 6, 1800

250. *A Defence of the Use of the Bible in Schools American Tract Society*, 1820.

251. Thomas Jefferson

252. William Pierce

253. Jeremiah Wadsworth, Letter to Rufus King, June 3, 1787

254. John Adams
255. Said at the Constitutional Convention of 1787
256. November 19, 1822 letter to Robert Waln Jr.
257. *The Countryman*, November 22, 1787
258. Roger Sherman's *Almanac*
259. Articles of Association, 1774
260. Speech to Congress, August 19, 1789
261. Letter to John Adams, July 1789
262. *Considerations on the Nature and Extent of the Legislative Authority of the British Parliament.*
263. Charles Page Smith, *James Wilson Founding Father 1742–1798.*
264. First Lecture, 1804
265. Lectures on Law, 1791
266. Lectures on Law, 1790
267. Lectures on Law, 1791
268. The Natural Rights of Individuals, 1804
269. Speech to the Pennsylvania ratifying convention, 1787
270. *The Dominion of Providence Over the Passions of Men*, May 1776
271. Eulogy for John Witherspoon by John Rodgers, May 6, 1795
272. http://www.trinityfoundation.org/journal.php?id=27
273. Ibid.
274. *The Dominion of Providence Over the Passions of Men*, May 1775
275. *Ibid.*
276. Sermon to New Jersey congregation, 1776
277. Thomas Jefferson
278. Rev. Charles A. Goodrich, *Lives of the Signers to the Declaration of Independence.*
279. Ibid.
280. Last Will and Testament of George Wythe
281. Ibid.
282. This was Wythe's personal motto, which he translated from the Latin, "*Secundis dubiisque rectus.*"
283. Letter to John Adams, 1785
284. From a ruling in the Virginia Supreme Court of Appeals, 1833

SELECTED SOURCES

These books are all excellent sources for information about the Founding Fathers as a group, as well as individual men and women of the era. We also provide several titles for more information about specific Founders in each of the individual chapters.

- Abrams, Jeanne E. *Revolutionary Medicine: The Founding Fathers and Mothers in Sickness and in Health*. New York: NYU Press, 2013.
- Adair, Douglass. *Fame and the Founding Fathers*. New York: Norton, 1974.
- Anthony, Carl Sferrazza. *America's First Families: An Inside View of 200 Years of Private Life in the White House*. New York: Touchstone, 2000.
- Benardo, Leonard and Jennifer Weiss. *Citizen-in-Chief: The Second Lives of the American Presidents*. New York: HarperCollins, 2010.
- Boutell, Lewis Henry. *The Life of Roger Sherman*. Chicago, Ill.: A.C. McClurg and Company, 1896.
- Bruce, William Cabell, *John Randolph of Roanoke, 1773–1833*. New York: G.P. Putnam's Sons, 1922.
- Burns, Eric. *Virtue, Valor, & Vanity: The Inside Story of the Founding Fathers and the Price of a More Perfect Union*. New York: Skyhorse Publishing, 2011.
- Ellis, Joseph J. *Founding Brothers: The Revolutionary Generation*. New York: Vintage Books, 2002.
- Encyclopedia Britannica. *The Founding Fathers: The Essential Guide to the Men Who Made America*. Hoboken, New Jersey: John Wiley & Sons, Inc., 2007.
- Franklin, Benjamin. *Autobiography of Benjamin Franklin*. New York: Henry Holt, 1916 edition.
- Goodrich, Rev. Charles A. *Lives of the Signers to the Declaration of Independence*. New York: William Reed & Co., 1856.
- Jay, John and Sarah Livingston Jay. *Selected Letters of John Jay and Sarah Livingston Jay: Correspondence By or To The First Chief Justice of the United States and His Wife*. Jefferson, North Carolina: McFarland and Company, Publishers, 2005.

- Kitman, Marvin. *The Making of the President 1789: The Unauthorized Campaign Biography*. Grove/Atlantic, 2007.
- Kostyal, K.M. *Founding Fathers: The Fight for Freedom and the Birth of American Liberty*. Washington, DC: National Geographic Society, 2014.
- Leidner, George, ed. *The Founding Fathers: Quotes, Quips, and Speeches*. Naperville, Ill., Cumberland House, 2013.
- McClanahan, Brion. *The Politically Incorrect Guide to the Founding Fathers*. Washington, DC: Regnery Publishing, 2009.
- Morris, Richard B. *Witnesses at the Creation: Hamilton, Madison, Jay and the Constitution*. New York: Holt, Rinehart and Winston, 1985.
- Nelson, Craig. *Thomas Paine: Enlightenment, Revolution, and the Birth of Modern Nations*. New York: Penguin Books, 2007.
- O'Brien, Cormac. *Secret Live of the U.S. Presidents: What Your Teachers Never Told You About the Men of the White House*. Philadelphia, Penn.: Quirk Books, 2004.
- Rappleye, Charles. *Robert Morris: Financier of the American Revolution*. New York: Simon and Schuster, 2010.
- Rees, James, with Stephen Spignesi. *George Washington's Leadership Lessons*. Hoboken, New Jersey: John Wiley & Sons, 2007.
- Rush, Benjamin. *The Selected Writings of Benjamin Rush*. Edited by Dagobert D. Runes. New York: Philosophical Library, 1947.
- Smith, Charles Page. *James Wilson Founding Father 1742–1798*. Chapel Hill: North Carolina UP, 1956.
- Stillé, Charles J. *The Life and Times of John Dickinson, 1732-1808*. Philadelphia, Penn.: The Historical Society of Pennsylvania, 1891.
- *Time Magazine. Thomas Jefferson: America's Enduring Revolutionary*. New York: Time Inc. Books, 2015.
- Winter, Jonah. *The Founding Fathers! Those Horse-Ridin', Fiddle-Playin', Book-Readin', Gun-Totin', Gentlemen Who Started America*. New York: Atheneum, 2015.
- Zinn, Howard. *A People's History of the United States: 1492-Present*. New York: HarperCollins, 2003.

INDEX

BOOKS BY STEPHEN SPIGNESI

- *Mayberry, My Hometown* (1987, Popular Culture, Ink.)
- *The Complete Stephen King Encyclopedia* (1990, Contemporary Books)
- *The Stephen King Quiz Book* (1990, Signet)
- *The Second Stephen King Quiz Book* (1992, Signet)
- *The Woody Allen Companion* (1992, Andrews and McMeel).
- *The Official "Gone With the Wind" Companion* (1993, Plume)
- *The V. C. Andrews Trivia and Quiz Book* (1994, Signet)
- *The Odd Index: The Ultimate Compendium of Bizarre and Unusual Facts* (1994, Plume)
- *What's Your Mad About You IQ?* (1995, Citadel Press)
- *The Gore Galore Video Quiz Book* (1995, Signet)
- *What's Your Friends IQ?* (1996, Citadel Press)
- *The Celebrity Baby Name Book* (1996, Plume)
- *The ER Companion* (1996, Citadel Press)
- *JFK Jr.* (1997, Citadel Press)
- *The Robin Williams Scrapbook* (1997, Citadel Press)
- *The Italian 100: A Ranking of the Most Influential Cultural, Scientific, and Political Figures, Past and Present* (1997, Citadel Press)
- *The Beatles Book of Lists* (1998, Citadel Press)
- *Young Kennedys: The New Generation* (1998, Avon; written as "Jay David Andrews")
- *The Lost Work Of Stephen King: A Guide to Unpublished Manuscripts, Story Fragments, Alternative Versions, Oddities* (1998, Citadel Press).
- *The Complete Titanic: From the Ship's Earliest Blueprints to the Epic Film* (1999, Citadel Press)
- *How To Be An Instant Expert* (2000, Career Press)
- *She Came In Through the Kitchen Window: Recipes Inspired by The Beatles & Their Music* (2000, Kensington Books)
- *The USA Book of Lists* (2000, Career Press)
- *The UFO Book of Lists* (2001, Kensington Books)
- *The Essential Stephen King: The Greatest Novels, Short Stories, Movies, and Other Creations of the World's Most Popular Writer* (2001, New Page Books)

- *The Cat Book of Lists* (2001, New Page Books)
- *The Hollywood Book of Lists* (2001, Kensington Books)
- *Gems, Jewels, & Treasures: The Complete Jewelry Book* (2002, QVC Publishing)
- *Catastrophe! The 100 Greatest Disasters of All Time* (2002, Kensington Books)
- *In the Crosshairs: Assassinations and Assassination Attempts, from Julius Caesar to John Lennon* (2002, New Page Books; 2016, Skyhorse)
- *The Evil 100* (2002, Citadel Press, written as "Martin Gilman Wolcott")
- *Crop Circles: Signs of Contact* (with Colin Andrews), 2003, New Page Books)
- *Here, There and Everywhere: The 100 Best Beatles Songs* (with Michael Lewis), 2004, Black Dog & Leventhal)
- *The Weird 100: The 100 Most Bizarre Paranormal Phenomena, from Alien Abductions to Zombies* (2004, Kensington)
- *American Firsts* (2004, New Page Books)
- *What's Your Red, White & Blue IQ?* (2004, Kensington)
- *Dialogues: A Novel of Suspense* (2005, Bantam Dell, 3 editions)
- *George Washington's Leadership Lessons* (with James Rees, Executive Director of Mount Vernon) (2007, John Wiley & Sons)
- *Second Homes for Dummies* (with Bridget McRae) (2007, Wiley)
- *From Michelangelo to Mozzarella: The Complete Italian IQ Test* (2008, Citadel)
- *Native American History for Dummies* (with the Smithsonian's Dorothy Lippert) (2008, Wiley)
- *Lost Books of the Bible for Dummies* (with Loyola's Dr. Daniel Smith-Christopher) (2008, Wiley)
- *The Third Act of Life* (with Jerome Ellison), 2009, Smashwords Edition)
- *The Titanic for Dummies* (2012, Wiley)
- *Grover Cleveland's Rubber Jaw* (2012, Penguin)
- *The Third Act of Life* (with Jerome Ellison), 2012, E-book Edition)
- *635 Things I Learned from The Sopranos* (2016, BearManor Books)
- *Droppin' Things You Never Knew About the Founding Fathers* (2016, Skyhorse)

ABOUT THE AUTHOR

STEPHEN SPIGNESI is a writer, university professor, and author of close to 70 books on popular culture, TV, film, American and world history, the paranormal, and American Presidents. He is considered an authority on the work of Stephen King (5 books), The Beatles (3 books), and the *Titanic* (2 books).

Spignesi — christened "the world's leading authority on Stephen King" by *Entertainment Weekly* magazine — has worked with Stephen King, Turner Entertainment, the Margaret Mitchell Estate, Ron Howard, Andy Griffith, the Smithsonian Institution, George Washington's Mount Vernon, Viacom, and other personalities and entities on a wide range of projects. Spignesi has also contributed short stories, essays, chapters, articles, and introductions to a wide range of books. He is the author of four of the acclaimed "For Dummies" nonfiction reference series, and also a novelist whose thriller *Dialogues* was hailed upon release as "reinventing the psychological thriller."

Spignesi has appeared on CNN, MSNBC, the Fox News Channel, and other TV and radio outlets. He also appeared in the 1998 E! documentary *The Kennedys: Power, Seduction, and Hollywood*, the A & E *Biography* of Stephen King that aired in January 2000, and the 2015 documentary *Autopsy: The Last Hours of Robin Williams*.

Spignesi's 1997 book *JFK Jr.* was a *New York Times* bestseller. Spignesi's *Complete Stephen King Encyclopedia* was a 1991 Bram Stoker Award nominee. Spignesi is a former Practitioner in Residence at the University of New Haven in West Haven, Connecticut where he teaches English Composition and Literature and other literature courses.

He lives in New Haven, Connecticut. His website is www.stephenspignesi.com.